MILROY WAS THERE

94TH Infantry Division Veteran of WWII Shares His

Battle Thoughts of Days in France and Germany and

Other Experiences in His 90 Years on this Earth

Memoir of John R. Milroy

petroy@charter.net

Milroy Was There

Published by
Sarge Publications
866-878-2096

Printed in the U.S.A. by
Allegra Alpena
(formerly Model Printing Service)
829 W. Chisholm St.
Alpena, Michigan 49707
www.allegraalpena.com

ISBN 978-1-60307-248-9

DEDICATION

Written for Joyce Ann Petersen Milroy, Jan Milroy, Michael

Milroy and Kathy Clark and their Casey and Brianne,

and Timothy Milroy and Vicki Milroy and their Andrew

and Elizabeth, and James and Lori Milroy and their Erin and Ellen

CONTENTS

PREFACE

This is a story about my life, part of it. I am not about to report the many stupid things that I did, or said, or thought. I am quite sure no other person was harmed by those things and I am thankful for that.

We all have a story to tell and now, with the aid of a computer, we ought to tell our stories. Now to tell a good story, an interesting story, it is best to embellish things a bit. The readers will appreciate a little amplification or exaggeration. I don't know how to do that well. I want to tell the truth as I remember it, so what I write may be more boring than I want this to be. It will be the truth.

Almost all of my working years after college have been in the banking business. I always thought that it was important to be honest, trustworthy, truthful and full of integrity in order to be a sound banker. The current national economy leads me to believe that one word has guided the path for leaders of most financial enterprises, and that word is GREED. I am glad that my career ended in 1990 as I turned 65.

I take full credit for all that follows and any obvious mistakes were mine to correct.

After the war ended, I just wanted to forget the whole thing and I didn't feel very special about the experience since over 12 million men and women are reported to have served in the military service. I knew I was no hero, just a survivor, and it was time to get on with my life. I even dropped my GI insurance, and that was dumb.

The 94th Infantry Division Association held its 60th Reunion in May 2009, in Nashville, Tennessee. Now I have attended several, but my first official one was in Dearborn, Michigan in 1986. I have really enjoyed these gatherings, held in interesting places and with well negotiated rates for room and board. About twenty men show up each year from L Company of the 376th Regiment, and this includes men who were replacements. When we left the states, a Company was about 200 men and a Division was about 15,000 men. Replacements are reported to have totaled about 10,000 men.

The Division History book reports that over 1,200 were killed or missing, 4,684 wounded and 5,028 developed frozen feet or other foot problems - 10,957 total from the original 15,000. I had no problems and therefore was involved in whatever "action" L Company was in. Some good fortune, eh? Replacement casualties were 7,000 maybe.

Most of the men at the reunions are men I really didn't know well and most of the replacements, not at all unless they happened to have been in our platoon, a group of about 40 men. But, I have really enjoyed getting to know these men, their wives, children and even grandchildren. Most of what I will be reporting is from my memory, although I have read much that others have published, the 94th Division History, the 376th Regimental History, Colonel Benjamin E. Thurston's book titled Ugly Duckling, Leon C. Standifer's "Not in Vain", as well as his

"Binding up the Wounds." William A. Foley, Jr. has written "Visions from a Foxhole" and he painted a large mural placed in the Boston State House that depicts General George Patton presenting a medal to an officer of the 94th as the Commanding General, Harry J. Malony looks on in a battle scene environment. "On being an infantryman," written by my friend Stephen B. Wood, and "Unfinished Journey," written by another friend, Kerry P. Redmann, are two other treasures of mine.

Col. Arthur Payne, former commander of the 376th Infantry Regiment in World War I, is shown speaking to the cadre and leading citizens of nearby towns at the activation ceremonies September 15, 1942 at Ft. Custer, Michigan. He is flanked by Maj. General Harry J. Maloney, Division Commander (left) and Brig. General Louis J. Fortier, Division Artillery Commander.

BRUCE - NORDA - BOB

JOHN - NORDA - BOB

JOHN

NANCY - BRUCE

2

I turned 18 on July 7, 1943, and it wasn't long after that my Draft notice arrived. I did not volunteer as many did. I had graduated from Kalamazoo Central High School in January and had completed a semester at what is now Western Michigan University in Kalamazoo, Michigan. I was sent to Detroit, Michigan to be inducted. Some of us enjoyed the Gayety Burlesque festivities and returned to Kalamazoo a Private in the army. On October 14, I reported at nearby Ft. Custer to be given my new GI clothing and other things, and soon was sent to Ft. Benning, near Columbus Ga., for 13 weeks of Basic Training.

The ASTP, or The Army Specialized Training Program, had accepted me as a member. The program was, we were told, to be sent to a college or University for two years of study in engineering and to graduate as an Officer in the U.S. Army, all of this after Basic Training was done.

Rather than try to remember and report on much during the 13 weeks at Ft. Benning, I hope that the two books of Redmann and Standiffer will be read. These describe very well what I experienced in Georgia from October, 1943 to February, 1944.

When we completed Basic Training, rumors began to float that the ASTP program was about to fold up. I was assigned to attend Washington State University in Pullman, Washington, but the ASTP program did collapse. Author Stephen E. Ambrose in his book, "Citizen Soldiers", reports on page 275 "…So suddenly there were 190,000 of the best and brightest of the Army's inductees from 1942-43", enough for more than ten divisions, available for assignment. Ambrose reports that about half were sent to Infantry Divisions, and reports indicate that about 3,000 were sent to the 94th Division, then in Camp McCain, near Grenada, MS.

Many of the older members of the Division started their training in Kansas in the fall of 1942 and knew each other pretty well by February, 1944. We ASTP soldiers were told that the older guys were warned that when we arrived as "mama's babies" they had better watch out or we would take their stripes away. So we were not too popular in the beginning.

As a Private, I was assigned to the first platoon of L Company, 3rd Battalion of the 376th Regiment of the 94th Infantry Division. There was about to be a basketball tournament between all of the companies in the Division and I became a starter on the L Company team. I had been a substitute on my High School team as well as the freshman team at Western Michigan University (a College in 1943).

Basketball Company Champions Of 94th Infantry Division

Company L, 376th Infantry basketball company champions of 94th Infantry Division. From left to right, first row: Sgt. Albert Moraldi, Pfc. Walter Klekota, Capt. M. M. Martin, Jr., (Company Commander); Lt. Robert Leedle, coach; Pvt. John Milroy and Pvt. Steve Wood. Second row: Pvt. Robert McLaughlin, Pvt. James Werrell, S/Sgt. Bill Ray, Sgt. Raymond L. Kuntz, T/5 Charles Davison, Sgt. Kenneth Staab and Pvt. Morris Bull.

ATTACK

Division Cage Champions Are A Motley Crew

COMPANY 'L' 376th INF. — Last Friday night the boys who play basketball for Company L, covered their company and regiment as well as themselves with athletic glory. The Division Championship signals the final for this sport. Somehow the comrades of Kuntz, Davison, Milroy, Wood, Ray, Klekota, et al, find it difficult to look at these men as champions though now they are on top. Out on the court they look as ill assorted a combination as can come from the proverbial infantry. Victory makes them more incongruous.

Well-wishers who watched "Red" Davison got the impression of a quiet-spoken man who maneuvers on cat feet with 200 pounds of beef. Bill Ray is the tallest and the lankiest and looks like a running windmill. Milroy is medium sized, white haired and cherub-cheeked. This boy from the ASTP is shifty and quick on his feet. Klekota is a small and muscular man who has no compunction against cutting down opposing players to handy sizes.

The anomaly of the team is Wood. He is gaunt to the degree of ghostliness; yet he run himself almost ragged on the court plopping in those sho shots. While Davison guards the basket and takes the enemy rebounds, Milroy, Kuntz, Ray, Klekota zig-zag across the flo to sink the enemy under a flur of points. The only man who not afraid of defeat or worri by his opponents' capabilities that confident flash prosaical named by his parents Ray Kunt called more descriptive names the men in his squad.

This athletic pearl, proud, d dainful, and handsome, sa "Dose bums were clumsy b belly dancers. Why we even be dem 11 to 10 on poisonal fouls say nuttin of de achual poin Now let me sleep to recover stren't."

Which is the Sergeant Ku way of saying "We made it, b barely."

The Division tournament started and we won our first game. After the game, the mess sergeant served us steaks back at the company dining facilities- not bad. Then we won the next game, and again we enjoyed some more steaks. The night of one game I was supposed to be taking a night infiltration course. In this test, men crawl on the ground under live machine gun fire with simulated mortar shells exploding near. I had done this drill in the day time. Well, that night I played in a game rather than take the test. We won that game too. We won the whole tournament and had our picture and write up in the Division newspaper and it seemed to me that we were quite popular with our fellow company men. For years I thought my new popularity was that we had made our company proud to be in this victorious Company.

Then, in the early 1950's some New York college basketball players were caught "shaving points" during their basketball games. This means if the bettor's line was that a team should win by 15 points, some players would bet on the games and purposely miss shots or do other things so their score would be lower than the betting point spread, though they still would win the game. This got me thinking for the first time that maybe bets were being waged on the Company L games in the 94th Division tournament.

In 1974, as I flew from Ft. Dodge, Iowa to the new job in Alpena, Michigan, I knew that a 94th Division Association was having an annual reunion at a hotel on North Michigan Avenue. Since I had a five-hour layover in Chicago, a cab took me to the hotel. Since this was only 29 years since I had seen these Veterans, I wasn't surprised that I knew as many as I did including the Mess Sergeant who had fed the players after the tournament games, those delicious steaks. He invited several of us up to his room for a drink and conversation. Soon the talk got to the basketball tournament. "Were you guys betting on the games," I asked. They looked at me as if to say, "You fool", and said, "Of course we were betting on the games - we bet the whole company treasury". So, after all these years I learned that my new popularity had nothing to do with Company pride in our victory but just plain old money in their pockets. I was, and am, a bit naive.

In the spring and summer of 1944 we did various kinds of training, most during the day and some at night. One week we were in Holly Springs Forest, north of Grenada, and did patrols and fighting against a make-believe enemy. We were tested to become the first Expert Infantry Regiment and Division. We learned about the various snakes in Mississippi and also chiggers; little red bugs that hid in your skin and itched like crazy. Naturally, we trained to shoot our rifles and throw grenades, and took long marches with a very heavy backpack, rifles and steel helmets. At times, there were shorter, faster hikes with a much lighter backpack.

We were given some weekend passes and once, I met my mother and sister at the Peabody Hotel in Memphis, Tennessee where we had a great time. Before going overseas, I got a pass for a few days so I could return to Kalamazoo, Michigan for a farewell meeting with my family and a girl friend.

Then, the rumors started. We were headed somewhere. We filled our duffle bags with all our possessions and were soon on a train going somewhere. When we stopped in Cincinnati, we guessed we were headed for the Atlantic Ocean. By July 31, the entire 94th Division was transported to Camp Shanks, New York, and we now knew that we were headed for Europe soon. Before we set sail, we were given a day in New York. We saw the usual sights and I ended up at the Paramount theater with many screaming young girls watching and listening to Frank Sinatra sing.

Later, a few guys went to the Club Zanzibar to watch the famous Mills Brothers, perform. For drinks I ordered a Pink Lady, a drink I had heard my mother order. I felt the others looked at me like, "what is this?"

I was 19 now, two years short of drinking age in Kalamazoo, Michigan. My first beer drinking was when we partied after completing Basic Training in Ft. Benning, Georgia. We went to the Stage Door Canteen and did see drummer Gene Krupa, but no other movie stars or famous people. As the train took us to New York, the Empire State building did not appear as high as I thought it would. I must have thought it would disappear in the sky.

It took some time to get us loaded on the Queen Elizabeth, all fifteen thousand and more. On August 6, at 7.30 A.M. we sailed the Hudson River and out into the Atlantic. My sleeping quarters were down in the bowels of the ship in a canvas bunk, with a bunk below and two above - tight quarters. The ship was to cross the Atlantic unescorted, so portholes were blacked out and no smoking was permitted on the decks at night, so German submarines couldn't see us. Two meals were served each day and we stood in lines for hours. Abandon ship drills were held and we were supposed to carry our

RMS Queen Elizabeth

WW II - Troop Ship Queen Elizabeth

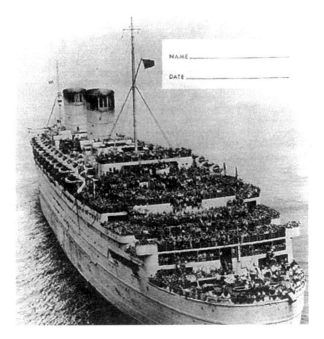

SLEEPING ARRANGEMENTS FROM NEW YORK TO SCOTLAND

life jackets or wear them, and we did exercises. The ride was smooth and we entered the Firth of Clyde on the 11th at Greenock, Scotland, near Glasgow.

Naturally there were crap games happening and my friend, Al Moraldi helped his friend run a game. Al has told me that his friend earned over $20,000 - quite a sum for 1944, but when we left the ship his money was impounded to be returned after the war. He tells me his friend was given his money back when he returned to the States.

As we debarked the ship, we were greeted by the sound of bag pipes and the men playing wore traditional kilts. We soon were on trains headed for England and I recall beautiful green fields and hills, and a clean looking landscape. We spent some time getting more training and were given a weekend pass to London. The famous government buildings were something to see, and changing of the guard. We saw the Wax Museum and made it to Hyde Park where there was shouting as men were making crazy speeches. We heard the German Buzz bombs coming in and exploding and later saw some of the destruction. At night, as I walked around, the "ladies of the evening" approached me and I just laughed. I thought I was supposed to be faithful to my last girlfriend in Kalamazoo and that stuff was for when I married. Religion had nothing to do with my decision and Aids wasn't even heard of, although we had been warned about "clap and syph." I wrote home about this event and have that letter. More mature guys probably enjoyed the girls.

Next we were loaded on ships to cross the channel to Utah Beach and landed 94 days after D-Day. No shots were coming our way. We climbed down ropes to a landing ship and were soon on the sandy beach.

As we left the beaches on foot, we saw evidence of the battles - crashed air planes and gliders, burned out vehicles and more. The first night we were in a farmer's field which was closed in by hedge rows. We had to keep our eyes out for cow droppings before we put up a pup tent. The hedge rows of dirt, stones and growth were built up over years to six feet or so, and therefore kept the animals in the fields. I have read that as our troops fought in France, tanks and other vehicles had a very tough time trying to move through these hedge rows.

Soon we were loaded into trucks to take us to positions near two sea ports, St. Nazaire and Lorrient, on the Atlantic Ocean. The Germans numbered over 50,000 and these ports were being used to

Post War Queens. Elizabeth sinking in Hong Kong, Mary
Accessible for tourists at Long Beach, Ca.

AP Photo

This once was a queen

Once the largest luxury liner afloat until she was ravaged by fire in January, 1971, the Queen Elizabeth is now this blackened hulk in Hong Kong harbor. The white frame of the ship's swimming pool is visible in the stern section at left. Marine experts say it is unlikely this queen will ever float again.

10

repair their submarines. We were told our assignment was to relieve another unit which was there to make sure the German troops didn't try to break out and rejoin other forces in France.

For several months, we went out on patrols looking for Germans as they were on patrol too. We did capture some and some of our troops were wounded and killed here. We were not to do any major attacking and had no objective to drive the Germans out of these two sea ports, but we were responsible to keep their troops there.

My first night in combat is very memorable. We were sent to an area called "Foret du Grave," located about fifteen miles East of St. Nazaire. This was a wooded area and probably had been a France Province park. This place was nick-named "The Spider" because at the center was a place where many roads from many directions all came together, and kind of looked like a spider with its legs intersecting. Our squad was sent to a road where troops we replaced had built covered dug-outs which would hold several men. There were places to look down the road for German soldiers on patrol, kind of an opening so one or two could be on the lookout while the other men could rest until their turn to be on guard duty. But, it happened that there was no room for me and one other guy. We were sent across the road where there was a ditch which we could hide in to spend the night.

In the middle of the night, I woke up and suddenly saw the reflection of the moon on the metal of a rifle, maybe being carried by a German. My heart pounded. It happened that as I sat, my rifle was on my lap, and I was afraid to move it to a firing position for fear the German would hear or see it. I sat petrified. Soon I heard firing and even the sound of mortar shells being launched - it seemed like a battle was happening. After a while, I decided I was imagining the German with a rifle. Probably others were having first night jitters as I was, and maybe there were no Germans out on patrol. Although, I later learned that there might really have been Germans moving nearby.

Several months in France were spent hiding out many places; sometimes in abandoned French farm houses, where we could cook a stray chicken and rest. More often we were in a fox hole or a larger dugout with others. We were sent out on day and night patrols looking for Germans. We did see them and captured a few. One memory I have of the small French villages is seeing piles of manure in front of the houses, and the smells made it clear what the piles were. As time passed the cold fall nights arrived, and frost was soon on the ground outside our dugouts. Our personal hygiene wasn't good, so often we got "GI trots," or diarrhea. Of course when the Germans shelled us, the fear of that didn't help a guy's insides. We didn't change clothes much and we didn't have the opportunity for many showers. Also, many of us carried a spoon in a shirt pocket for eating, right next to an oily rag which held a tooth brush for cleaning our rifles. As I was bending to climb out of a placement one morning as it lightened up, needing to move my bowls, I didn't make it. That was the end of the underwear seat. In December, I wrote home that we all now had body lice, so showers and clean clothes arrived along with some white powder that was suppose to kill the critters, or at least keep them away.

When it came time to leave France, we had been shot at, shelled, went out on patrol, got sick or were quite uncomfortable. Many men were wounded and a few killed. The Division history book reports that there were 719 casualties during roughly three months. Later, in Germany, the casualties were ten times greater in a shorter period of time. Both authors Standifer and Redmann, for his brother, report they were wounded in France.

One beautiful fall day in France, I was alone in a dugout on guard duty at the edge of a field, west of a farm house where other guys were. I had a paperback book which I was reading, glancing up occasionally to look for the enemy. We never had any activity there so I sat and read quite comfortably. But, as I looked out in front one day, I saw two guys walking toward me a few yards to my right. At first I thought they were French farmers because there was much farming going on in front of us even though there was a war going on. But they might be Germans. There was a wooded area to my right and these men seemed to be headed there. I saw no German helmets, but as they neared the entrance to the wooded area I raised my rifle and had it pointed on one man who was not too far away. I wasn't a great shot, but if I pulled the trigger I am quite sure that he would have been hit. What I would do about the other guy I didn't know. Well, if they were French I didn't want to pull the trigger so I did not. However, soon after I did hear shooting to my right and I was told later that others had captured the two Germans.

The experience in France was about to end. I had many scary experiences, especially the shelling, but all in all it hadn't been too bad there. Often there were rooms where we could write letters home and some guys played cards. Some got passes to town and, one night as they returned, they offered to share a wine bottle. On my passes I had learned about "Vin Rouge" and "Vin Blanc" and never consumed too much. But when these guys handed me the wine bottle, I took a big slug. I gagged, could hardly swallow, my face got hot and I couldn't talk. Well, these guys pulled a trick on me, as the liquid was Calvados and maybe a cheap one too. Needless to say, I didn't drink any more from that bottle.

Next we were headed up to the front lines somewhere in Germany.

We packed up all our belongings and were loaded into trucks. Our first stop was at Chateaubriant, France. In a big field, slightly dusted with snow, we erected a pup tent. Each soldier has in his backpack one half of a tent, so you paired up with another guy who had his half and his ropes and stakes. Vince DeMase from Buffalo, New York was my partner. We had a heck of a time, but we finally had our tent. The next day many of us were loaded on a train, a "Forty and Eight" - famous trains of World War I, which held forty men or eight horses. There was straw on the floor, no heat and no facilities except a bucket in case a soldier couldn't hold it until the next train stop. Then we unloaded and headed for the handiest place to "do our business." The Division History book states that our ride took us south of Paris and near Verdun, famous battle ground of WWI. The trip ended at Thionville, France, somewhat south of Trier, Germany, and southeast of Luxembourg City. Soon the weather became severe and years later we learned that the 44'-45' winter was the worst in decades.

Initially, we were billeted in farm houses and some of the rooms were used for the cattle. I think the animals helped warm the house but the smell was overpowering. As recent as the 1990's, on a trip to Europe we learned there still are farm houses where cows sleep near the family.

Soon it was time to begin fighting on the east side of the Moselle River near Remich, Luxembourg. It was January 14, 1945. In the morning dark, we walked from Wochern, Germany, to positions in a wooded area west of Tettingen and Butzdorf, Germany. We were to be in a support position as others attacked the village of Tettingen. We would be there in case help was needed by the attacking units. At this point, I was a 19-year-old PFC scout for the platoon of forty men. A scout walks ahead of the platoon looking for the enemy and maybe

Marshalling area for the St. Nazaire Sector forces in the vicinity of Châteaubriant

Headed for
Germany,
on 40&8 cars,
pup tents at
Chateaubriant, Fr.
Passed Chartes,
France on train.

These 40+8 trains
are what we rode
to Germany in.

They could hold 40
men or 8 horses.

drawing fire from them if the Germans see the scout first. This is not a great assignment. Based on the experiences in France and that "war," I had a book in my hip pocket to read when the skies became light as we waited in our reserve position. But then my squad leader told me to find a position outside of the woods to be on the lookout for a German patrol. Soon after, when it was still dark, I heard our artillery open fire on Tettingen with a heavy bombardment. This was all new to me, and this half hour of softening up of the enemy was unbelievable. The noise and the lights were awesome.

No Fourth of July display of fireworks I have witnessed since made such an impression on me. When it grew light and the shelling was over I saw the soldiers marching to attack the village. I also noticed a fox hole near me, dug by a German I suspect, and filled with snow. Soon, the Germans began to fight back and I heard their rifles firing as well as mortar shells landing in Tettingen. This went on for hours and I got used to the sounds of battle.

Suddenly I heard a new sound of some German artillery coming from a different direction. Then, "whoosh" shells landed on our wooded reserve position area. I dove for the fox hole I had spotted and it was wet and cold. The sounds came out of the woods from the men who had been hit with shrapnel, cries for help. Some had been killed. No fox holes had been dug, so soon I heard the sounds of men digging with the shovels we carried. Time went by. Then, some hours later, I recognized the sounds of the artillery that would be coming our way, and the shells landed again in our woods. More cries rose from our men. While fox holes had been dug, there was no time, nor the materials, to build a cover to protect the men from the "tree bursts," which sent the metal shrapnel downwards. More were wounded and dead. The Officer in charge of our platoon was wounded with his guide and my sergeant who sent me out of the woods was wounded and died later in a hospital. Many more were wounded and killed in this shelling.

Morris Redmann, whose home was in New Orleans, La., was in the same basic training company in Ft. Benning as I and he was in the same platoon of the 94th as I. He helped a wounded soldier who was hurt in the first shelling and returned to that same spot and was killed in the second shelling that afternoon. Years later I learned that Morris had graduated from college and was in law school at age 18 when he was drafted. He was a brilliant man. Years later, one of his younger brothers, Kerry, attended two of the 94th Infantry Division

STANTON GRADUATED WITH ME, JAN. 1943

HIGH HONORS

Stanton Keith Barnes   Philip Warren Mange

John Robert Milroy

HONORS

Theodore Lula Coolis   Wade Van Valkenburg, Jr.

Robert Bayer Ingling   Dorothy May Walsh

WAR MEANS DEATH

"Alles Kaput!"

Pvt. S. K. Barnes War Casualty

Killed Fighting with Gen. Patton's Army.

Pvt. Stanton K. Barnes, 19, was killed in action with General Patton's Third Army Nov. 17, according to a telegram from the war department received by his parents.

Pvt. Stanton Barnes

Mr. and Mrs. Harold E. Barnes, 311 West Inkster avenue, Monday night. He had been overseas since August and was a member of an infantry regiment of the 95th Divi-

nen up the draw east of Butzdorf, to locate the German mortars which ad been firing from that vicinity all day. This latter patrol reported n its return, that the enemy had withdrawn from these positions

16

Association Reunions to learn more about his brother's experiences and details of his death. Kerry wanted to write a book about Morris which included most of the letters that had been sent to the family in New Orleans. I sent some things to Kerry and got to know him pretty well at the reunions, by letter and by phone. Kerry mailed me a draft of his book and before he died I got a copy of the finished product.

Morris was probably the most brilliant man in the ASTP program. What a waste of a life. He was buried in Europe. Kerry took a trip there with the son of WWII author Stephen Ambrose, and visited the grave. Kerry conducted a religious service at the gravesite.

This day ended and nobody could have been any luckier than I to have been sent outside the woods to be on guard duty. Now the next day it was our turn to go on the attack. Reading later, I learned that our Battalion Commander worked out a plan for our attack on Nennig, Berg and Weis. Engineers early in the morning were to clear a path of mines near a rail road track which when completed we were to follow just before the attack, once again in the early morning following our shelling of the little villages. Our history books report there was mass confusion in our attack. Some platoons were sent in the wrong direction and one was captured, but later was freed. I fired at the enemy but I doubt if I hit anyone. Late that afternoon we proceeded door to door while grenades were thrown into the basements. Near a garage I recall David Fairbrothers working his way around to the opening and seeing a German, at whom he took a shot. Dave was suddenly thrown on his back, I think because his rifle was filled with grit and the recoil caused this. The German had an advantage but he surrendered to us. Maybe the concussion from David's close range shot confused him or maybe he was just ready to give up. I often have thought that we were both very lucky that the German didn't get us first. We spent several nights in houses hiding from German patrols and hoping that their shelling didn't hit our roofs. We were sent away to rest and learned that the troops that replaced us had to deal with a bitter counterattack.

Next we were to learn about German Schu-mines. These little wooden boxes held gun powder, no shrapnel and were hidden under the snow. If our soldiers stepped on these mines or tripped them in any way, the explosion could blow a foot off or at least mangle the foot, arm or whatever body part hit the mine. Being wood, mine detectors could not find these small boxes.

It was time for our unit to leave the rest area and we were to lead an attack against the Germans. In the dark we were taken to a tank trap and, with the help of small ladders, we climbed through the trap and were ready to start the attack. It wasn't long before we were in an area filled with Schu-mines and our guys began stepping on the mines. Many men were hurt badly and it wasn't long before the Germans started firing machine guns and started shelling us. Somebody discovered a communication ditch that the Germans probably had built and we ran for cover. Some of us made it. As we ducked down in the trench we could avoid the machine gun and rifle fire, but we could only hope that the shells landed somewhere else. It sounded and felt as though the shells were coming right down on our heads, but they missed. I thought later that since we were at the apex of a hill, the shells may have been very close but just missed and hit the ground at the bottom. Had we been on flat land, I think those shells would have destroyed us. Naturally, since we were supposed to be the leader of the attack and we were pinned down and very confused, another unit had to pass through us and take over the leading of the attack. When it turned dark, we were sent back to regroup and find out our next assignment. Years later I read reports that many of the men with mangled feet, or had their feet blown off, stated that they felt they had a million dollar wound since they were headed home and would not be killed or have a more serious wound.

As we returned through Nennig, we saw stacks of German bodies lying in the snow. It was reported that some time later, Germans found these bodies and for propaganda purposes had Axis Sally say on the radio that we had lined their soldiers up and shot them in a mass killing. She referred to the 94th Division as "Roosevelt's butchers." In truth, both sides were waiting for "grave details" to gather the bodies for gravesites. You can't blame the details for waiting for the area to be safe to enter.

I think it was at this time that I was sent back to a field hospital to get rid of the high fever I had acquired. The rest of our outfit went back to rest and get ready for another attack. The medical folks helped me get well in a hurry, but while I was there we were given some decent food and, one noon, were even entertained by a musical group. I also had a personal experience which stayed in my memory. When I was able to get up and head for the can, I found that the facilities were in a separate cement block building and all there were to relieve oneself were round holes in the cement floor, no toilet seats or standing urinals. So, as I was squatted down, in came a cleaning lady with a bucket and mop. She was nice enough to pretend like she didn't notice me, but this 19-year-old was very embarrassed. In a rather recent trip to Europe, my wife and I discovered that it isn't unusual today for members of the opposite sex to be doing their cleaning while the facilities are being used.

While in the hospital, I received a report that I had been made a "buck" sergeant and put in charge of a twelve-man squad on February 2, 1945. Once recovered, I returned to our unit to find it was still in a rest mode but getting ready for an attack the next morning. Technically, this meant I was one of the few that never missed a day of combat, was not killed or wounded and never got trench foot or frozen feet. About 5,000 of our men did suffer - the winter was very cold. Many of the men wounded or afflicted by foot problems were sent back and never returned until the war was over. These numbers coincide with the reports I heard later that we had needed about 10,000 replacements to fill our ranks.

The next morning we started another attack and we gained some new ground - not much, but some - and we dug our fox holes. While we carried cans and boxes of food and more was sent to us, on occasion a vehicle called a "weasel," which had tracks rather than wheels, could make its way through the difficult terrain to bring us food from the kitchen which was well back from the front lines. This food was almost hot and much tastier than the cold packaged stuff of K and C Rations. With the cold weather we sometimes had two guys in a hole so that one could try to sleep while the other was on guard. All alone, a guy might freeze to death.

For whatever reason, on February 15th, 1945, our 376th Regiment joined the 10th Armored Division. Up until this point, most of us had never seen a map. We hardly knew what day it was and where we were headed other than a hill in front us, or some other land mark. We carried a compass so we could know directions but we had no knowledge of overall plans or strategy. Dates and places have come from the various books I have. Now that we had vehicles - tanks, trucks jeeps, etc, once we broke through the German lines, we could move greater distances until we reached a new German strong point. Sometimes we got a ride, and one day it is reported that we covered 23 miles in two days to the village of Ayl near the Saar River. Our next assignment was to cross the Saar and take the territory up some steep hills which were filled with many Germans in cement pill boxes and other defense positions.

We learned later that 3rd Army Commander, General George Patton had a bunch of reporters in Ayl to watch our crossing. Before we could cross our Company Commander, Capt. William Brightman was killed and the Regimental Commander, Colonel Harold H. McClune was wounded seriously. Many others were killed and wounded. In the first platoon of L Company, our Lt. Robert Foster was promoted to Company Commander to replace Capt. Brightman and I was put in charge of the platoon, I think as a Staff Sergeant. The attempt to make the crossing during the day time to please General Patton was a disaster. We made our way down to some flat ground through an orchard near the Saar River bank and down on the ground to wait for the engineers to deliver the boats for crossing. Also, other engineers were supposed to fire up a smoke machine which would hide us from the Germans looking down at us from the hills on the other side of the river. There is criticism of Patton in William Foley's book and he is very outspoken about this on a DVD Film of Patton. In addition to the Patton movie is a documentary disc with No. 2 being "Patton's Ghost Corps." This DVD came out in 2006, and our Division had interviews taken at a reunion by the California filmmakers. I am in that film for two seconds but Foley makes a big speech, saying that too many men were lost because of General Patton.

Back to the actual Saar River crossing: The smoke machines did not work, and if the boats indeed got there, some reports later state that the Germans could see the boats and were able to destroy all of them. When dark came we made our way back to Ayl and awaited new orders. While the original plan was for L Company to lead the way, now we were in the rear. We crossed at a different place and we made it at night with no problem. We climbed the hill and didn't see any pill boxes on the way up, but when we reached a road we found an empty pill box which was large enough to hold what was left of our platoon. By radio communication I was told to climb the next hill and find the flank of another unit at the top. I was to make a plan to put my platoon from there back to the pill box so we could be protecting the north flank of the battalion as it made its way east at the crest of the hill. I took Bill Lehfeldt with me, about the only other guy left from our original platoon, the rest being replacements, and took him up the hill. As we worked our way back we determined

The Valley of the Saar, looking upstream from the vicinity of the Staadt crossing. In the distance, upper left, are the cliffs opposite the Hamm Bend which is located in the left center of the picture.

As enemy shells burst near them, men of the 376th Infantry work their way across open ground preparatory to moving into the bridgehead

where we would leave our platoon in various places to guard the flank of the battalion. Then, the platoon followed us up the hill and we dropped two at a time in the guard lookout spots. The last three men we left on the road about fifty yards from the pill box we had occupied and where our radio was. Why I wasn't ambushed that night as I thrashed around is a wonder because we later learned there were many Germans there.

The next day I was ordered to gather the men and return them to the pill box. So, up the hill I went. As I found the men I pointed the way back and finally I came to the three men left on the road. Only, I found one German soldier dead and two of my men dead. Later, I found the third back at the pill box. He told me that in the night, they heard someone walking down the road and they thought it was me. The German got too close and only the third guy was able to duck and then kill the German. The fallen men had been new replacements. I hardly knew them and, to this day, I don't recall who got the grave detail to them. While we were doing this guard detail, the rest of the battalion had tried to work its way to the crest of the hill, only they were surrounded by Germans. I have read that a small air craft dropped food and ammunition and other supplies to sustain the battalion, and finally the Germans were killed and captured. For a few days we occupied Ockfen, at the base of the hills as the Division was building bridges and getting tanks and trucks across the Saar.

The entire Battalion was now headed east by foot, single file, following paths through the wooded hills. One duty of the lead platoon of a company was to fan out and hopefully discover if there were any Germans lurking who could let some of us go past and then ambush others following. One day, my platoon was the lead one, leading the whole single file line of about 600 men in the Battalion. At one point we reached the edge of a wooded area. Our direction took us across an open field and then back into another wooded area. I sent two scouts across the open field to see if they drew any enemy fire. They didn't, so the rest of us crossed to the next forest. As I entered the woods, I suddenly saw my men hit the ground as though they had spotted something. When I got to them they pointed to our left, or north, and I spotted a German apparently looking out on guard. Why he hadn't seen us I will never know, but I started walking toward him with my rifle cradled in front of me. Suddenly he turned toward me and I began firing from the hip, not a recommended way to fire the rifle. I missed, but he ducked down and then back up he came with a white flag of surrender and several more Germans came out of the placement to surrender. Then, as I proceeded through the woods, I saw the men up front all hit the ground, as something was wrong. When I got up there, a whole flock of Germans came up out of well-camouflaged fox holes, all holding their hands up to surrender. It turned out that they were all either very young boys or old men, by army standards, and had been sent out from their nearby village to protect it. I believe if this event had happened a bit earlier, when these guys thought the war could still be won, they would have shot us. But they were ready to give up. I could have taken a gun as a souvenir, but we had been trained not to do that. If we were later captured, those holding German property would be dealt with more severely. So these captured men dropped their weapons and I suspect that guys in the rear probably picked them up.

Out of the woods, and on mostly flat land, we suddenly were off to the races headed for the Rhine River. We went through village after village, to find white flags of surrender on flag poles or hanging out of windows. Sometimes we were walking on the edge of Hitler's famous Auto-Bahn highways, and sometimes riding in trucks. Often we saw bloated horses by the roadside; these had been pulling German vehicles.

We saw their tanks and trucks and artillery tipped over and destroyed and thousands of their unarmed soldiers marching to our rear. Soon we were on the edge of a very large city on the Rhine, Ludwigshafen. However, the war was still on and we observed too many German civilians, probably having just shed their uniforms, who we think were sending information to their troops up ahead. We had to watch some of our tanks start to drive over an open area and get destroyed by German weapons, probably the famous German 88's. I knew we were about done fighting, but I was as frightened as almost anytime. As we walked down the big streets, there were too many big buildings where German snipers could hide and shoot us easily. But we made it.

Here I was alive, never wounded and never acquired frozen feet or trench foot, in one piece. Also, I later thought about what had not happened. While fighting, the Germans never took the land back that we had gained. That did happen to some troops that replaced us. I saw and heard German tanks, but they never shot at our group, nor

23

did I have to hide in a foxhole as they drove over. That did happen to others. I never had to attack a German pill box, nor feel I had to duck from their guns. While I always carried grenades, I didn't throw them much. Never tripped a Schu-mine. Never had to fire a flame thrower, although I received training and did fire one then. At first we carried bayonets, but never used them, nor had them used on us. Poisonous gas was not used by either side where we were. I wasn't captured. Never had to view the bodies and living skeletons in a concentration camp, but others in our Division may have had to. I had no psychological damage, although at our reunions some claim they are still suffering from Post Traumatic Stress Disorders. In March, 2009, the army decided that no soldier can earn the Purple Heart due to PTSD.

I did get shot at and shelled. I did shoot at Germans but I don't think I hit anyone. I was one lucky soldier.

Next we were headed north to leave the Third Army, Patton's, and to become part of the Fifteenth Army. On March 26, 1945, we were back on the "40&8" cars going to the Dusseldorf industrial German area. The war was still going on and though it was possible that some Germans, in civilian clothes, might try to harm us, we really didn't worry about that.

Now we had to be part of helping to get the German lives in order in occupation duties there. We did do some state-side training and marching and some parades were held. We first lived in German houses and were ordered to avoid fraternizing with Germans. That really meant we were to stay away from the fraus and fraulines, or women. Many guys ignored those orders, including officers in our company. Women were brought into the houses to spend the night, and one older non-officer enjoyed humping his girl for all to see, especially as he stopped for a moment to light a cigarette and then resumed activities for all to see. Parties were frequent and some bad liquor consumed, and one guy managed to fall down some stairs a bit drunk, and ended his days there.

There were many "displaced persons camps" filled with people from many different countries. They had been forced by the Germans to work in their production plants, thanks to Albert Speer, a favorite of Hitler. Their living conditions were poor. One day my platoon was sent to a camp to be on guard to protect the people from the Germans, and often from themselves. When we arrived, since I was in charge, I was to meet their camp leader. This man came to me with a drink and black bread. We couldn't communicate (I don't know what his nationality was), so it was an awkward moment. I was concerned about drinking the unknown concoction but I ate the bread. That was poor diplomacy on my part.

One of the young men was from Greece and he taught me how to perform the card trick, "Three Card Monte." I got rather good at it. Down through the years, unscrupulous people have fleeced money from others doing this trick. Three cards are shown, and with a deft maneuver, a card is thrown down which seems to be another card and a bet is made to see if the sucker can name the card. Often a shill assists the card shark and seems to guess the right card and collect his bet. Then, when a real bet is on, the "shark" does the maneuver and collects his winnings. If by chance it appears the sucker is about to guess the right card, the shark knocks the table over and the trick has to start over. In our European trip in the 90's, we saw crowds where this trick was being done to the tourists.

The time came for my platoon to be sent to guard a prison in Wuppertal, Germany. The units we replaced had taken all the weapons away from the German prison guards but they, and all the other prison employees, were still running the prison. We put one man with a rifle at the center of the prison, but if the unarmed German prison staff had wanted to take control they could have done that very easily.

The three-story building had three wings. One wing held real German criminals. Another wing held German political prisoners, but we let them all go. Then another wing we began to fill with our political prisoners. There was a US Intelligence Officer at the prison who interviewed the prisoners to see which ones we should keep locked up. One prisoner was a former SS man, and other Nazis were rounded up. One tried to commit suicide in his cell.

Each day I went to our political prisoner wing with a German guard and we were taking role to be certain they were all still locked up. We would knock on the door and say "vie heissen sie?" meaning, "what is your name?" The prisoner might say "Schmidt" and I would say "forename," for the first name. If the answers were correct we would move on to the next cell.

At one of the 94th Reunions the guys told me that when I was called to go back to Company headquarters, they pulled out some wine and had a nice party. I thought I knew what was going on and had some control but I guess I didn't.

25

I got my souvenirs at the prison. I took a German Walther police pistol, 32 caliber, and an army belt and buckle, a weapon cleaning kit, a "cat of nine tails" with evidence that it held metal nails at one time, and a German helmet. I put my home address on adhesive tape and stuck it to the helmet. It arrived in Kalamazoo, Michigan safely. I held no special skill with most weapons, so I got a kick out of being able to disassemble and reassemble that Walther pistol quickly. When back in Kalamazoo I registered the pistol with the police, bought some shells and fired it once. Then I hid it in my duffel bag with the other souvenirs, and had the bag in the attic. One day two granddaughters found the bag, and the pistol. I know it was not loaded, but others have thought the same, only to have an accident. So, I decided to rid our home of all guns, which meant the pistol as well as two shotguns which I never fired in Alpena, Michigan.

On June 13th, 1945, orders arrived to raise my rank to Tech Sergeant, the role that I had been playing for months. The next day we were back on trucks headed first for Austria, on the way to Czechoslovakia and a village called Vodnany, south of Plzen. The war ended in Europe on May 6th, 1945, and on May 19, the Commandeering General of the 94th Division pinned the Bronze Star to my jacket. He asked me where my home town was and when he learned it was Kalamazoo, he remarked that he had enjoyed the Park Club there when he had been stationed nearby at Ft. Custer. The Club was a place for the elite of Kalamazoo.

On April 30th, 1945, I was sent to Paris, France on a pass. There we did a lot of walking, although I am sure we received some truck transportation. I am sure the mass transit system was not functioning, and I don't believe the Eiffel Tower was open for tourists. The Red Cross provided our housing and food, but we found the open bars on our own. We were near the Place de La Concorde and had a group picture taken there. Naturally we found the Arch de Triumph de L'etoile and walked the Champs Elysees and toured the Notre Dame Cathedral, where I bought souvenirs. I mailed my mother and "girl friend," or pen pal, some perfume, and my sister an ink well (she wasn't too happy about that).

We visited the risqué Place Pigalle, and attended the Folies Bergere, where the girls wear very little clothing. The Moulin Rouge was nearby and I later learned that this area was the Montmartre Quarter and the Basilica of Sacre Coeur was also there.

On our trip from Germany to Czechoslovakia we traveled through Nuremberg and stopped to walk the stadium where Hitler made speeches to huge crowds. Albert Speer had much to do with staging these events.

Vodnany, Czechoslovakia was a small farming community, very neat and clean. The farmers lived in the village and went out to do their farming. There were no fences around a plot of land. Our unit first lived in large tents, but soon we occupied a building which may have been a school at one time. When we visited the local bars for a beer, we found bright, highly polished tables, tasty pastries available, no smoking and families with young children enjoying themselves. It was just a nice, wholesome atmosphere.

The war in Japan ended in August, 1945, and the older guys in our outfit had earned enough points to be sent back to the States. To keep us busy, we rose early to trumpet sounds and trained doing activities like close order drills and cleaning our weapons. All of this as though the army planned on us staying in as a career.

We also went out in the field to do other training which included having platoon leaders like me giving classes on various fighting tactics. We really mostly sat around smoking and talking. However, one day I was in for a big surprise when my platoon had an unexpected visitor. Third Battalion Commander Benjamin Thurston presented himself without warning. I had seen him often in combat; he was up on the front lines and most men with his rank stayed back, I think. We had never met officially, but I sure knew who it was and I really respected him. I pretended that we were on a break between my lectures, but he just stayed there. I had to call the platoon together so I could start another lecture, but I had no idea what I was going to talk about. So I started talking and as I made some point the Colonel interrupted me and began to expand on the point. Then he said "good work Sergeant," and departed. What a relief. In later years, I decided that he knew what was really happening, and not happening, when I was supposedly giving lectures, and he just bailed me out. Years later we were encouraged to write letters to our aging leader, and we exchanged many letters. Once, I visited West Point where he graduated in 1926 and I secured a copy of the page in his year book that had his picture and remarks about him. I mailed this to him and he was happy because he had lost his copy in a barn fire years earlier. Later, when he wrote a memoir that he titled "Ugly Duckling," he asked that a copy be sent to me and I have it.

27

A few years ago on TV, a report was given of that year's West Point graduation exercises and he was shown as the oldest graduate there. I tried to get a copy of that to send to him, but I failed.

In the summer of 1945, Bob Hope visited our unit in Czechoslovakia. He had Jerry Colona, the mustached comedian, and Frances Langford with him. We were outdoors in a big field and that was fun. I also was given the opportunity to be in a high school auditorium to watch the famous singer and actor, Paul Robeson perform. He had as his pianist, Eugene List, who also was a famous artist.

That summer we were also visited by General George Patton. Our platoon had practiced a stunt using long logs, and a squad of twelve men to each of three logs. We lifted them up and kind of tossed them around and did more. When he stopped to watch us perform, he asked me something, but I was so nervous I am not sure what I said back, but he moved on. He was killed that November in a freak accident as he was being driven to a game-hunting event.

On July 4th, 1945, a group of us, about 600, were trucked to Plzen, to participate in a parade. We were left at the town square where there were many multi-story buildings on three sides of the square, and a huge Cathedral at one end. A large crowd was there, including many people leaning out of the building windows. We were placed next to a crack Czech Drill team about our size. In front of us was a temporary stage where speeches were to be given. The first dignitary was President Benes, who had been in exile during the war. The Czechs were given the command to "present arms" and all lifted their rifles in front of them to the proper place. Our group was given the same command. We, of course, were not a drill team, rather a bunch of "Citizen Soldiers" as author Stephen Ambrose called us in his book, just waiting to go home. We presented the rifles in good order. Then the command was given to "order arms" and the drill team hit their rifles simultaneously and in the end, hit the butts of their rifles on the road with one sound, as though 600 of them were just one man - a great sound. We were trained to start hitting the rifle with one sound, and we did, but we were to rest the butt of the rifle on the ground with no noise. You could guess what was about to happen. Our guys decided to copy the Czechs and hit the butts of their rifles on the road. Six hundred rifles hit the road at various times, not one clean sound but rather a bit like a machine gun, *bang bang bang*. As each new dignitary was presented it happened again,

PILZEN JULY FOURTH PARADE 1945

29

GENERAL PATTON REVIEWED 94ᵀᴴ DIVISION IN CZECHOLOVAKIA

[handwritten: the space to be when he reviews our company my platoon]

This photo, which has appeared several times in the Attack, was published in the Auburn University Alumni News in December 1982. It shows General George Patton reviewing 94th troops in Czechoslovakia, July 1945, while riding in a 94th jeep bearing the name "War Eagle." The Alumni News editor wondered (in print) if perhaps Patton might have been a War Eagle, which is the official motto of Auburn Alumni. The Attack received the photo news clipping from Bob St. Clair 2/Hq/301, Chattanooga, TN, who asks if anyone knows who dubbed the jeep "War Eagle" and why. If you should know, write to the Attack and it will be passed on to Bob St. Clair and the Auburn Alumni News editor.

LOG   DEMONSTRATION FOR   PATTON   I AM THIRD FROM RIGHT IN FRONT

only worse each time. I felt I could hear the crowd laughing at us. We marched out, the Czechs with no base drum and no officer calling cadence, marched step by step while we, with a drum and cadence, were way out of step. I was embarrassed for us. Many years later I decided we were really showing our strength - the fact that we are a country of individuals, not all following orders of others. Maybe. I bet our Drill teams would have performed very smartly had they been in our place. In 2008, at the tomb of the Unknown Soldier in Arlington Cemetery, we saw the performance of the guards on duty and they could perform on any drill team.

While in Czechoslovakia, I was given a weekend pass to a famous spa called Marienbad. The buildings were nestled in beautiful wooded places and there were mineral baths to take, great food and very comfortable sleeping arrangements. There were ping pong tables and other games, just a great spot. Maids cleaned the rooms and made our beds. One morning a maid offered to find me a nice young girl to spend the night. Stupid me, as in London, I convinced myself that this was not to be my behavior at this point in my life. I had never joined a church, so it had nothing to do with religious beliefs. Oh well, to each his own.

In October, 1945, I received a telephone call from Glenn Allen Jr. of Kalamazoo, Michigan. Actually, the call was coming from the 94th Division headquarters in Czechoslovakia where Glenn, as an attorney, was a judge advocate. I had known Glenn fairly well, mostly on the tennis court. He said he was headed back to Kalamazoo to be with his ailing father and he wondered if he could carry any message from me to my parents. Nice guy. After the war he became Mayor of Kalamazoo, and then continued on to political jobs in Lansing as State auditor, and later as a judge in the State Court of Appeals. Some years later he was interviewed by a Kalamazoo Gazette reporter doing an article about Glenn's career. He told how in 1945 he had campaign literature printed in Czechoslovakia to send back to Kalamazoo as he prepared to run for political office. I realized he was doing a good political job in his call to me and probably others. Good for him. In 2009, if you look for it, on Mackinac Island you will find a tennis court that he gave to the public, dedicated to his wife.

My letters that I sent home and were kept by my mother are not very interesting and really quite dreary. I was anxious to return home and was losing all of my older friends as they returned to the States. Our training was boring to me but I did find time to play on the company softball team and later on a basketball team playing against the Czechs. I did have a unique experience with the Czechs after the basketball games. Win or lose, we all shook hands, something my primary coach in Kalamazoo would never have encouraged us to do. Tennis players shook hands after a match, but in football, basketball, baseball and other team sports there was no display of such good sportsmanship. I enjoy seeing that today after our high school and college games - not all teams, but most.

At last the word came in. I was heading back home. A train took me to Lucky Strike, a camp near the Atlantic Ocean. On December 20, 1945, we boarded the SS Hood, a victory ship, tiny compared to the Queen Elizabeth. Our route over the northern seas was a rough one and some days we were not permitted to go up on the deck. The ship rolled and many of the guys became deathly ill. It was a thrilling 11-day trip, and as we floated by the Statue of Liberty in the New York harbor it was New Years Eve for 1946. When we debarked we had a brief stay at Camp Kilmer, visiting New Brunswick, N.J. one night. Then I was sent to Indiana and Camp Atterbury where I was handed my honorable discharge papers and some mustering out money. I slept overnight on a bench in a Chicago train station and the next day arrived in Kalamazoo, Michigan.

My "girl friend" and 27-month pen pal was about to graduate from Kalamazoo College and marry her new friend and I was headed for Western Michigan College to pursue a degree. In what, I didn't know. When I left the States in 1944, I really wasn't sure I would return from Europe or Japan, so I gave no thoughts about any future career. I have a friend in Michigan, a retired dentist, who developed frozen feet and ended combat in January, 1945. We were in the same company in basic training at Ft. Benning, after entering the service at Ft. Custer at the same time. Not too many years ago he was elected president of the 94th Division Association. Later he was the prime mover to get the state and federal governments to dedicate part of I-94 near Ft. Custer to the 94th Infantry Division. When he was interviewed, we learned that when he was recovering in England he held a responsibility which brought him close to the unit's dentist. He spent day after day watching the dentist at work and talking with him and made his mind up to be a dentist, and that is what he became. I see him a great deal at the reunions and enjoy him and his wife very much. Isn't it interesting that fate or whatever from his war experience sent him to his life's work?

Lenka Jandova, now Mrs. Zdenek Sroubkova, is my friend living in Pilsen, Czech Republic. We have been corresponding since the late 1970's and Joyce and I were with her in Prague in 1993 and in Berchtesgaden, Germany in 1998.

When we arrived in Alpena, Michigan in August of 1974, we soon learned about Stanley Beck, a highly regarded teacher, school administrator and business man. He led the Junior Achievement program for the high school and I enjoyed his leadership of that. We learned that we had some WWII experiences to share and one day he asked that I give him a copy of the chapter in my 94th Division History book which discussed our duties occupying part of Czechoslovakia in 1945. It seems that Stan had written a museum in Czechoslovakia inquiring about something and the lady responding had asked him for some information as she was writing a paper about the U.S. occupation for some college work. The lady was Lenka Jandova, married, with daughters Kristyna and Petra. Then, at Christmas and Easter, she mailed Stan and me a beautiful card with a brief message in English. I began mailing her things that I thought she might enjoy.

Before Stan died, a nice crowd watched Stan being honored in the high school auditorium as this place was named for Stan. A curtain was lowered to display his name on the wall to the right of the stage. I wrote to tell Lenka that this had happened and later to inform her of his death.

When Joyce and I took a group tour to Europe in 1993 I wrote Lenka to tell her that we expected to be in Pilsen and I would try to call. It happened that when we reached the square where I had been in the parade in 1945, there was no place to park our bus. Maybe Czechoslovakia was not prepared for tourist groups. I must admit that as we drove into that country, the buildings and general area were not as neat and clean and buildings as nicely maintained as those in Germany, from which we were driving. The tour group moved on to the hotel in Prague where we were scheduled to stay. The hotel was a beautiful modern building on the edge of very old buildings, most of which seemed to be suffering from neglect due to the war and Russian occupation.

Once settled in our room I went to the lobby to ask for help to telephone Lenka at her home in Pilsen. When the lady reached her and tried to get Lenka to talk with me, Lenka would not, apparently not sure that her English was adequate. So, the lady just said, "she says hello."

LEARA JANDÓVA
ZDENĔK ŠTROUBEK
ŠROUBROVÁ
8/6/98 BERSTESGARDEN GERMANY

With friends from Czechoslovakia, picture taken in Germany

That was a disappointment. We ate and then enjoyed an outdoor fashion show. I had never been to such an event but I really enjoyed watching the beautiful, young, curvaceous ladies strut their stuff.

As we reentered the hotel lobby, a young lady came to us and said "she will be in the lobby at 11 p.m." No names were given but I guess we looked like the right tourists. We sat down and waited, and as the "witching hour" approached, whenever I saw a young lady arrive at the check-in desk, I went up to ask if she was Lenka. After several negative responses I noticed a young couple who might be the ones. The lady responded, "Yes, I am Lenka." What fun. It turned out that she and her brother-in law, who would be the interpreter, had borrowed a car and had driven a difficult hour to reach us from Pilsen. The restaurants were closed but a bar was open so we spent more than an hour of interesting conversation. All they wanted was U.S. Coca Cola to drink. Before they left we got pictures and she needed help with her verbal English, maybe the notes and letters I received for years were written with assistance from others. As years passed, I kept receiving cards at Christmas and Easter.

In 1998, Joyce and I enjoyed another European bus tour. This time we missed the Czech Republic, but I mailed our itinerary to Lenka. One day we arrived at Berchtesgaden, Germany, where we had been on the first trip and this famous area once was where "The Eagle's Nest" was constructed by Hitler's underlings to honor his fiftieth birthday, I think.

When I went to breakfast the next morning, the hotel manager told me a message had arrived from Lenka to state "we will be there at 4 p.m. if it is convenient for you." I didn't know if "we" meant her and her husband or them and their two daughters. Before 4 p.m., we sat on the front porch to look for their arrival. A car arrived, and Lenka got out and with her a man.

She introduced us to her friend and they joined us on the porch for a Czech beer. We learned that she had divorced and later that both her parents had died that same year. She gave Joyce a piece of pottery and we had a great talk and ate dinner at the hotel. Lenka's ability to speak English was now very proficient. She married Zdenek the next July 3, and took Lenka's two daughters on a trip to Zermatt and that beautiful mountainous area where this trip took us. We finally got a computer in January 2004, and I have been able to share e-mail messages with Lenka. This has been great for me to have a friend thousands of miles away. She mailed me a copy of the book she wrote and this past year when some of us received a medal from the Czech Republic, she helped explain what was written on the medal. This is something very positive that came to me from WWII.

The 94th Infantry Division Association Reunions have also been very rewarding. Earlier, I wrote about the few hours at the Chicago Reunion of 1974. My first official one was in Dearborn, Michigan in 1986. I have been to thirteen more since, including the 60th held in May of 2009 in Nashville, Tennessee - thought to be the last, since the original thousands who returned to the States after the war has dwindled to an estimated 1,200. At the Reunion in 2008, there were almost 200 vets there and another 300 or so wives, widows, children and grandchildren. If there are to be more gatherings it will be because the newly formed Alliance will assume responsibility for this. I did attend the 2009 Reunion and there will be one in Charleston, S.C. in 2010 which I will miss.

In Dearborn, the highlight was to see Bill Lehfeldt, once the guide, or Sergeant, in the same platoon as I, as members of L Company, of the 376th Regiment. Bill went on to a fascinating career with the U.S. State

Department. He became an expert on the Middle East and was stationed there for some time. After he retired he was hired by G.E. to be their expert on the Middle East. He and Mariella have attended several reunions, bringing two sons and a daughter to at least one reunion. He was elected president of the 94th Association for 2002-3 and has been asked to be MC several times since.

John Kelton was a sergeant in my platoon and after the war he made a career of trying to get L Company veterans to attend reunions. He sent letters, telephoned and with his friend Martin Evans actually called on men at their homes to urge them to attend. This was my first opportunity to listen to Rev. Manning give the Saturday morning speech where he states the 94th was one of the best Infantry Divisions in the whole army. The listeners all felt very good about themselves. How many years he has given this speech I don't know, but he gave another in May 2009.

In Baltimore, MD, in 1987, I met Al Moraldi and Vincent "The Count" Cinque who were old buddies from training days in Kansas in 1942. Al had been on the L Company winning basketball team with me in 1944. The Count had been in my platoon, and when he returned to the outfit in Czechoslovakia after an injury, he was a buck sergeant, subordinate to me, and he thought that was funny. When he returned to the States, he made a point to contact my parents to let them know that I was okay. Later, I roomed with Moraldi in Kansas City, and then with the "count" in Atlanta.

These two were with John McCarrell, and he got a great kick kidding me about being a banker. As a union man, he was a 30-year president of Local 54 at the Fisher Body plant in West Mifflin, Pennsylvania. He said he was on a board of a large UAW credit union. He also claimed he had a great deal to do with the creation of the UAW Educational Center near Onaway, at Black Lake, north of Alpena. I later learned that he gave an important seconding speech for Richard Nixon at the Republican convention in Florida in 1972. As a Democrat union man, he had attended only Democratic Conventions before, so he received much publicity as a Democrat for Nixon speaker. This is the same guy who Moraldi helped run a crap game on the Queen Elizabeth going to Europe in 1944. So at last I had met a really "big wheel".

In Niagara Falls at the 1994 Reunion, I met Mark and Jennie Romohr who own a huge farm near Lincoln, NE and are ardent University of Nebraska football fans. Mark was a Replacement soldier and told me that when he arrived, he was told that I was the only one left in L Company of those who left the States in August, 1944. When the war ended he was sent to Nuremberg, Germany to be a guard over the Nazi war criminals.

Also at this reunion, Bob and Peggy Anders had their daughter there and when she learned that I was a CEO, she had fun kidding me based on her experiences with other CEO's who really didn't know anything or do much. Al and the Count took me to my first "off-track" betting place. The Count really liked to gamble.

The Reunion in Kansas City gave Al and me the opportunity to visit Ex-President Harry Truman's home and other things in Independence, MO.

Since Al and I were sharing a room I learned a lot more about him and Ann, their daughter and son. For several years Al's grandson, A.J. attended our reunions, first as a young man and "gofer" for the gal managing the reunion. Al and Ann raised this boy and he became a fine young man. Al's main career was owning an in-city bar in Los Angles which was sold so they could retire in Palm Springs, CA. Our low attendance at this reunion may have been due to the death of

John Kelton on September 4, 1995.

The 1998 Reunion was in Atlanta, GA and Dr. Richard Kelly, my dentist friend from Northville, Michigan, was the presiding president of the Association. Lt. Robert Foster lives near Atlanta so he attended. He is the one who I replaced as Platoon leader as he had to become Company Commander due to the death of Capt. William Brightman. It was great seeing him again. The stories I heard from the Count as I roomed with him were fascinating. I never could have ever known him except for being in the Infantry branch of the service. Glen Moon and his wife Mary live in Marietta, GA. They recall growing up there when it was a farming area with few people and now almost a major city so near Atlanta.

L Company leader is now Arnold E. (Gene) Wise, following John Kelton. Gene has done an excellent job sending us new rosters and keeping us informed about men of L Company. He lives at Stone Mountain, Ga. So this Reunion was handy for him.

In May of 2000 we were off to Norfolk, VA. Charles and Alice Remmington were attending their first reunion. Charlie and I were great pals in Czechoslovakia after he returned from major shrapnel wounds. He was put down on January 27, 1945. After the war his career was spent in management for a telephone company in Pennsylvania.

Kerry Redmann was there to learn as much as he could about his brother Morris who was killed on the first action in Germany. I have written earlier about the book Kerry wrote. We enjoyed each other's company and one afternoon we entertained retired Lt. Colonel G. Phillip Whitman with his favorite libation. His stories were fascinating and I have the book he wrote after a life career in the military.

Steve Wood attended his first reunion here, purposely avoiding previous ones for thought-out reasons. Steve had been the star of our winning L Company basketball team. He lived in the Berrien Springs, Michigan area, not far from my hometown, Kalamazoo. After the war, Steve earned more than one degree from the University of Chicago and spent a career teaching at the college and University level, retiring in Kingston, RI. As a studious man, he wrote a paper which declared that after the futile efforts of our military to secure the French port at Brest, it would have been foolhardy to attempt to secure St. Nazaire and Lorrient.

Each reunion, a souvenir of some type is given to all. That year it was an apron for out-door grilling use. After putting mine, on Joyce took a picture which I mailed to Charlie Remmington. He wrote back that I looked like either Emeril Lagasse or Julia Childs in "drag" and he had the picture published in our quarterly Attack letter. I knew of Julia but I wasn't familiar with the famous Emeril of the Food Channel. Once I saw him on TV, I became a fan.

In 2001, the reunion was in Danvers, Massachusetts, not far from Boston. Joyce and I drove there and did much sight-seeing. Naturally we enjoyed Quincy Square in downtown Boston. One of our bus trips took the group near the shore so we could eat lobster there and bring some back to share with those that didn't take the trip. Joyce and I were able to visit the Kennedy Library as well as Harvard University, Lexington, Bunker Hill and more. I collected $400 winning the 50-50 drawing and gave half back later.

Knoxville, TN. was the site of the 2002 reunion. Bill Lehfeldt was president of the Association. Side events included going to a Country Western stage performance and stopping at Pigeon Forge, where Joyce and I have stopped often. We honeymooned at Gatlinburg in September, 1953 so this area is special for us. In recent years, this is Dolly Parton territory.

Houston, Texas was the place for the 54th Reunion in 2003. In 1951, as the Kalamazoo Chapter incoming president of the American Institute of

Banking, I was given a perk to attend the National Convention in Houston and I took my first air plane flight ever from Chicago. While we stayed at the Rice Hotel, convention headquarters, we made a point to visit the Shamrock Hotel, made famous by a wealthy Houston oilman. At the time it was considered a "folly", built so far out of town, so huge with its Olympic sized swimming pool. Movie stars were brought in to be seen at the pool.

All these years later, the location is in the heart of town. The hotel was torn down to make room for part of a medical complex. There is a sign that mentions this was the site of the Shamrock hotel.

On our tours, the empty Enron building was prominent but the company had folded. There was so much to see in that area. The Astrodome was near the convention hotel and the Reliant Stadium was nearly completed nearby. Downtown we saw the baseball stadium where W. Bush was owner of a team. The Rice Hotel still stood as condos. The mansions to the west seemed to have great numbers of men grooming the lawns and shrubs. One tour took us to the National Aeronautics Space Center and we were in the room which we all saw on TV many times. Another tour was to San Jacinto, the battle ground for Texas Independence. Sam Houston was part of that so he got a city named after him. History reports that it wasn't much of a battle.

Memphis, Tennessee was where the 2004 reunion was held. Al and Ann Moraldi joined me to eat ribs at the highly-recommended Rendezvous Restaurant. We rented a horse-drawn cab to see the sights near Beal Street and we had a drink at B.B. King's bar.

Two men from Hollywood were at the reunion's hotel and they interviewed over sixty of us about our WWII experiences. In the summer of 2006 their documentary DVD went on sale in a package which contained the Patton Movie and then several documentaries, one "Patton's Ghost Corp," which is parts of the interviews taken in Memphis. Moraldi and I are in the film, me for two seconds.

I took a cab to meet a guy that I roomed with in 1958 at the Rutgers Graduate School of Banking. This was a big surprise to him but it was great to meet the mature Norfleet Turner III, a wealthy guy I guess. His dad was the president of the largest bank in Memphis in 1958.

The Peabody Hotel was still in business. In 1944, when we got a pass to Memphis, we always tried to stay in that hotel. That is where my mother and sister stayed when they took a train from Kalamazoo to see me for a weekend.

Milwaukee, Wisconsin was the location for the 2005 reunion, the 56th. The highlight for one family was the celebration regarding the presentation of the Silver Star to deceased Capt. Macke, which his family had persuaded the government to confirm. He was L Company Commander for a brief spell. One night we ate at the famous German restaurant, Mauder's. We walked part of the University of Marquette's campus, saw Pabst Mansion Theater and the water front Art Museum.

In 2006, Joyce joined me in a driving trip to King of Prussia, in Valley Forge, Pa. We had to stop at Penn State University on the way. We were there in the 1950's. The Reunion tours took us to Valley Forge so we could hold the rail that General Washington probably held at his headquarters building. Another day we visited the Pennsylvania Dutch farming area and learned about that culture near Lancaster, Pa.

In Philadelphia we stopped at Independence Hall and saw the

Liberty bell. We spent much time in that historic area and went in the Episcopal Church which was the first in our new country.

On the way home we called on Alice and Charlie Remmington in Berwick, Pa. His eye-sight was failing so we were very fortunate to be with them before his eyes failed more. We were buddies in Czechoslovakia in 1945.

In 2007, Cincinnati, Ohio was the 94th reunion sight. The tour took us to the water and I visited the museum dedicated to the "Underground Railroad," which was the site where the blacks reached after being assisted by white families on the other side of the river. A personal event for me was to have the enthusiastic native woman narrator turn out to be a classmate of tennis great Tony Trabert. In the 40's I saw him play against Western Michigan in a basketball game and later I saw him winning tennis matches on TV. Joyce joined me on the edge of Washington, DC for the 59th reunion.

The trip was one of our best. Experiences at Pittsburgh were a great surprise and we must return. We managed the subway system to the heart of our capitol. We had tickets to walk through parts of the White House.

The organized tour took us to the Mall, and naturally Arlington Cemetery and the Changing of the Guards at the Tomb of the Unknown Soldier. Lincoln Memorial was inspiring, as was the new WWII Memorial.

Eating at the remodeled, huge railroad station was fascinating, realizing that this is where our elected officials for decades reached their destinations not far from the Capitol buildings.

The Fairview Park Marriott at Falls Church, Virginia was the site of this reunion. Bob Anders brought his son who was great to be with. His career with Waste Management has been a great one and his duties caused him to live in Australia a few years. We also spent quite a bit of time with Glenn Moon and his wife, and they are a great couple.

After the Reunion we visited Annapolis, Maryland, toured the U.S. Naval Academy and did much more. Then we drove on to Ocean City, Maryland on the Atlantic Ocean and enjoyed other new experiences.

The 60th reunion was held the last week of May, 2009 in Nashville, Tennessee. Since Rev. Manning was recovering from an operation, it was not easy for him to give the annual speech telling us how great we were in WWII. The Association decided to have another reunion next year in Charleston, South Carolina at a date near Memorial Day.

When this chapter started, I was getting ready for the service. I turned out to be a survivor - no hero, just a survivor, and what an experience the 27 months was. Attending The 94th reunions has been a great treat. I am kind of glad that I didn't have the time or the money to attend the earlier reunions. I have had few discussions about our experiences fighting. I have really enjoyed getting to know these men and women as civilians.

There is to be another reunion in Charleston, SC but that same weekend we will have the first opportunity to watch a grandchild graduate from college. James and Lori's daughter, Erin, will graduate from Ohio Northern University and she has already lined up an accounting job for next fall in Toledo, Ohio. First she must secure her CPA degree this summer of 2010. So, that may be the end of 94th reunions for me.

Picture taken in spring, 1946

I was born July 7, 1925, in Kalamazoo, Michigan at Bronson Methodist Hospital. My brother Bruce Denton was born November 9, 1922, and sister Nancy Lou, on July 16, 1926. The Roman Catholic Borgess Hospital in Kalamazoo was run by The Sisters of St. Joseph then.

Looking back eight decades, I have concluded that we were extremely fortunate to have grown up in Kalamazoo and that our parents did a great job of preparing us to enjoy and cope with the worlds we three would know. They brought many talented and caring people into our lives and introduced us to education, other culture, sports activities and much more.

Our father, Robert Rogers Milroy, was born Christmas Day, 1899, to William D. Milroy, a physician, in Chicago, Illinois. Our mother, Norda Rae Schoonmaker Milroy was born December 13, 1898, In Plainwell, Michigan. They met at Kalamazoo College where Norda graduated in 1920 and our dad was a few credits short. They married in January, 1922.

I don't ever recall our dad talking about his roots or even hinting that he was proud that his dad had been a medical doctor, although he was proud of the Milroy name. But, his dad died from typhoid fever when our dad was only seven, and dad's sister, Mary, had died earlier at three. The doctor's practice was then in Logansport, Indiana.

Dad's mother was born March 26, 1873, as Sarah C. Rogers at Bedford, Michigan near Battle Creek. She grew up there and studied music at the Normal Summer School in Detroit and became Supervisor of Music in the Public Schools of Delphi and Monticello, Indiana. She married Dr. William D. Milroy September 14, 1897. After his death she returned to Battle Creek to live with her mother. She married widower John F. Stough in 1913 and moved to Ross Township. Then they moved to Lawton to grow grapes where Ruth Laverne was born June 25, 1914. After a few years in Lawton and Kalamazoo they moved to the Henderson farm east of Galesburg and became active in the Methodist Church. In December 1933, they moved to Florida due to poor health of grandma and she died January 29, 1936.

Our father lived in Logansport, Indiana with Dr. Charles

Ballard's family and he graduated from Logansport High School in 1917. Some records indicate that our father returned to live in Kalamazoo where his mother, step-father and half-sister Ruth lived. With this background, it is clear that our father really had no role model as a father, so that role could not have been easy for him.

Our mother's parents, Ray Schoonmaker and Nora Bigelow were married in Plainwell, Michigan in May 1896. Ray ran a pharmacy and invented a laxative and other medical products as well as the "Schoonie's Scooter," a fishing lure. He died when I was very young so I have no memory of him. But, my grandmother, Nora Schoonmaker played a big role in my life. Her home was within 200 yards of the Eastern Campus of what is now Western Michigan University. She rented rooms to girls going to what was then Western Normal and this kept her attitude always young.

As I grew up, I spent considerable time with her as I was able to mow her lawn, pick grapes and climb her cherry tree to do some fruit picking. I did other chores around the house and she would holler "man on the floor" if I was on an errand upstairs where the girls were. When the girls were away at Christmas time, our family often stayed there to gather and celebrate with "Big Grandma" as she was called since her "little" mother-in-law lived with her. At dinner, Grandma insisted that she preferred the back of the turkey. Once I recall my uncles Mark Putney and Carl Schoonmaker playing a stunt on her by hiding a microphone in the basement so they could make announcements interrupting the radio program on the air. Uncle Mark especially liked to play practical jokes, which sometimes confused me.

At lunch time, as a youngster, I would walk to Grandma's to eat and take a piano lesson there. Grandma took up the cello in later life and she composed a hymn even later that the older ladies choir performed at their Methodist Church and in other gatherings. When our parents traveled to Florida in January 1936 to attend Dad's mother's funeral, we stayed at "Big" grandma's house for several days. That was a good time for us and we did some skiing on the hill there. Our skis had a leather strap that almost held any boot to the wood ski – almost, but it seemed as though we fell out of the strap frequently. We managed to miss the many trees that were on the hill. I was 10 at this time. This seemed like a vacation week while our parents were gone. Big Grandma's greatest contribution to the world was her three children.

I enjoyed watching Grandma beat her male neighbors in Chess, since these men were doctors, dentists and professors at Western. I believe her formal education was limited but her competitive juices were strong. She passed those desires to win on to my mother, and she to me. I never saw her unhappy about anything, nor treat anyone badly. She was just a real lady.

In recent years, genealogy has seemed to be more important to many people, including our daughter Jan. The book *"Roots"* may have had something to do with that as well as the invention of computers and the information available through them.

Have Milroys made significant contributions to the world? Not in the 20th or 21st centuries. However in the 1800's, folks in Indiana thought very highly of General Samuel Milroy, near Delphi, and his son Gen. Robert Houston Milroy of Civil War fame. Tracing back, John M'Elroy, Earl of Annandale was on the losing side in the Battle of Culloden when the English prevented Charles Stuart from regaining his kingdom. So, in 1744, John and his wife fled to Ireland and changed their name to Milroy.

Later the couple emigrated to Carlisle, Pennsylvania where Samuel was born in 1780. Samuel was a leader in the Constitutional Convention to form the state of Indiana in 1816. The museum in Delphi, Indiana has a great deal of information about Milroys.

In my years growing up in Kalamazoo, Michigan, men and boys didn't do much with writing diaries – that was a female thing. So, as I proceed, at 84, I am writing from memory. Psychologists used to inform us that the first five years of a child's life had the greatest impact on the kind of person we became, maybe they still believe this. I never have remembered much about that part of my life. So, the 12 years of what I do recall, until I turned 18, will be the events reported here.

Kalamazoo, with a population of about 50,000, was a great city to be in as I matured. Back then there were no malls, so all services were concentrated in the downtown area. The first house I recall was about five blocks south of the heart of the city. We walked to everything, although we always had a car, and never more than one. There was a streetcar line on Rose Street at the end of the court where we lived, but that service ended when I was very small. A City bus service started and the Upjohn Company had its own busses which brought employees to and from work. Airplanes served some people, but I don't recall knowing anyone who used them.

Music was important in our lives. My father had an excellent tenor voice and he practiced at home with mother at the piano. He was the Congregational Church soloist and he sang in the Messiah. I think my parents performed at dinners and other group meetings for money besides their joy in doing this. My brother and I were forced to become members of the St. Luke's Episcopal Boy's Choir. My first song to perform in front of the other boys was "My Faith Looks Up To Thee" and I was accepted. A boy started as a "prep" and soon graduated to be in the official choir. The director, Henry Overly, was in charge of all the music at Kalamazoo College. He was a stern man who demanded attention from us, no fooling around. This was serious business and serious music. We practiced on Tuesdays after school, Thursday nights with the adult men and women and Saturday mornings. Then for the Episcopal service we wore the usual garb with the help of the Choir Mothers. If your talent was good enough, a few were in The Singing Lads, who performed for women's guilds and for others. Each year the choir practiced strenuously to prepare for an annual evening concert which was performed in the Central High School auditorium, for a sold out crowd of over 2,000. The

St. Luke's Choir, Kalamazoo, MI
Blonde, Middle Front Row

46

choir sold tickets and if enough were sold, a boy could attend a week-long camp at Lake Michigan. We were actually paid small change for each practice session. I think we started at about eight years old and continued until our voice changed, which was thirteen for me. In the beginning, the Saturday time was no fun since I missed doing sport activities with my buddies. In the end I was very glad that we learned about serious music this way and I had some good friends in the choir.

My dad's second job was selling industrial fuel. This meant that in the good weather, he took customers to play golf at the Kalamazoo Country Club. He was on the course many week days and about lived on the course on weekends. In time he gave up singing at church so he could play 18 holes on Sunday mornings and another 18 in the afternoon with our mother and another couple. He probably began to enjoy his beer and Tom Collins drinks more in this environment. I was given lessons at about 8 years old and definitely learned the fundamental rules of never improving the lie of the ball in the rough and only in the fairway before "summer rules" were declared. We learned there should be no "gimmy" putts. Most amateur golfers don't worry about those rules, they may say they do, but if no one is watching, so what. How can you get a good score and win prizes and get your name in the paper if you follow the rules?

My dad's first job that I knew of was in the office of a local paper mill company. When he was manager of their company baseball team he brought the equipment and often, me, to the games. There was no 50-50 fund-raising then, they just passed a hat for direct donations.

From an early age, I recall being taken to many Kalamazoo College sporting events, football, basketball, track and tennis. I even learned to sing the school song and to know their cheers. K-College had very good tennis teams and one player "Buck" Shane was often the State of Michigan singles champ. Don Worth, Bill Culver and several others were excellent too. In later years, this team won over 50 consecutive conference titles. I got into the game early, won some championships, played on the Kalamazoo Central High School team, and in 1942, with Lee Koopsen, won the regional title and later in Ann Arbor reached the finals of the class-A double's team tournament. We lost that final match.

Tennis in Kalamazoo was influenced when the National Junior and Boy's tournament was moved here from Culver Military Academy in Indiana. The Stowe Tennis Stadium was built soon

47

Ball Boys for Tilden- Perry exhibition match in Kalamazoo

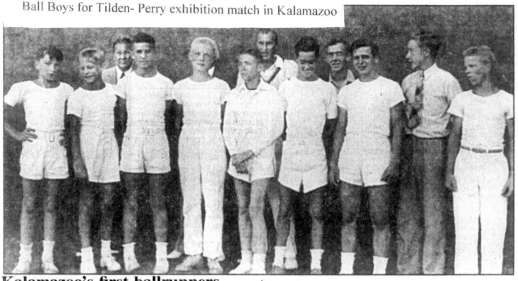

Kalamazoo's first ballrunners

Ballrunners are a familiar sight in the USTA Boys' 18-16 National Championships these days, but the first to ply their trade as ballrunners here was this group serving in support of the Bill Tilden vs. Fred Perry exhibition match on July 16, 1941. The photo, provided by Lee Koopsen, shows from left: Bob Espie, Harold Upjohn, Vinnie Richards, Jack Moreland, John Milroy, Tilden, Dick Barnes, Bob Stowe, Harry Parker, Paul Staake, Paul Riepma and Koopsen. The ballrunners were all outstanding young tennis players. Perry defeated Tilden in a long match, 5-7, 7-5. 11-9.

after, first with clay courts and later with a hard surface. There were several out courts and three in the stadium with a press box and some covered bleachers for hundreds of fans. Players came from Australia, such as Rod Laver, and others from all over this country. K-College's coach George Acker had daughters who played well and one was in the professional tournaments. I played in the tournament one year and was beaten soundly by a California player.

The golf course opened new social horizons and many new friends were brought into our house. Jack and Marge Dickson were two special ones and she became a good player, better than mother, who played well, and both got one hole-in-one. Often we met the Dicksons on Sundays for brunch at Milham Park. As we sat at some picnic tables opposite a par three water hole, we took bets on whether the players would hit shots over the water onto the green. Our laughing when they dumped the ball in the water was not appreciated, I am sure.

Western Michigan College had teams to watch, especially baseball, which produced excellent teams and some players who went on to have professional careers. Basketball teams were excellent too under coach "Buck" Reade. He initiated a new fast-break style,

48

Win Regional Tennis Crown for Kalamazoo Central

By placing two doubles teams in the regional finals here Saturday, Kalamazoo Central won the regional Class A tennis championship over teams that had won twice this year over the Maroons. Left to right, Leon Koopsen, Johnny Milroy, Pete Van Sweden, and Dick Boekeloo. Koopsen and Milroy beat Van Sweden and Boekeloo in the finals after all four boys qualified for the state meet June 6.—Gazette photo.

Milroy, Koopsen Meet Bay City Pair for Title

Benton Harbor Gains Eastern Honors; Maroon Golfers Busy.

DETROIT—(AP)—Play in the Michigan high school Athletic Association tennis and golf tournaments, regionalized because of the war, moved ahead on two fronts today.

At Grand Rapids, where Benton Harbor already has gained the Class A net crown in the western section, finals were scheduled in singles and doubles in this division and Class B.

Tigers Win Title

Benton Harbor gained the unofficial title yesterday when Richard Stolpe and Merle Brown gained the singles finals. Wesley Samborn of Clare won the Class C-D championship with a 6-1, 6-3 victory over Del Boersma of Holland Christian while Robert Fairchild and Richard Mieler of Frankfort gained the doubles title in this class by defeating Ed O'Brien and Harvey Bolch of Rockford.

Other finalists:

Eastern district: Class A doubles John Milroy and Lynn K. Koopsen, Kalamazoo vs. Jack Learman and Ed Weiss, Bay City.

Class B Singles

Class B singles Dave Dexter, East Lansing, vs. John Dudley, Trenton; Class B doubles Dave Rank and John Swanson, Marquette, vs. Albert Nadeau and Leonard Brumm, Marquette; Class C-D singles Fred Ott, Grosse Pointe St. Paul's, vs. Andy Paton, University High, Ann Arbor; Class C-D doubles Robert Crandell and Warren Hooper, West Branch, vs. Orion Johannes and Dennis Kiley, Standish.

Western district: Class A doubles Bill Coleman and Alex Martin, Grand Rapids Ottawa Hills vs. Jack Lipman and James Hansen, Muskegon Heights. Class B singles William Veining, Grand Haven vs. Paul Teske, South Haven; Class B doubles Dick Ford and William Haynes, East Grand Rapids, vs. Philip Springsteen and Clifford Moulton, Dowagiac.

Golf tournaments 18-hole medal play are scheduled today in each district.

In eastern district ... Ann defend Roger Lew... Arbor, champion, gained the fin ... singles meets Louis Rupff of Ba. City. Another 1941 winner, Fred Ott of Grosse Pointe St. Paul's, matches strokes with Andy Paton, of University high, Ann Arbor, in the Class C-D singles.

49

although when I first watched games there, after each basket made, there was a new center jump, no "fast break" then. Bill Gleason and I often sat on a hill which faced the football field at Western so we bought no tickets then. One year "Hap" Coleman from Hamtramck, Michigan was really fun to watch. He was very fast and shifty and scored many touchdowns after receiving punts and kickoffs. We watched many track meets too, and that was all free.

My first sport's influence was from Fred Zuidema, a Western graduate who directed the playground in the summer where I played. He also helped me learn to run, high jump and broad jump for the elementary track meets against the other schools in Kalamazoo. I won some events and ran on relay teams and one year the Kalamazoo Gazette reported about a meet and called me a "toe-headed midget speedster" as I won two dashes and I think was on a winning relay team. When I moved to Junior High School, so did Fred Zuidema as our coach in touch football and basketball. When I moved to High School, so did Mr. Zuidema as my first basketball coach and he became head football coach. He seemed to be a tough man but he was fair and kind. If we made a dumb mistake, he would say "well where there's life there is hope." We heard that a lot. He liked to spit in his hand as he talked to us and then rub the hand on his shirt at the same spot - his wife had a hard time getting those stains out.

Summers we spent a lot of days at nearby lakes of which there were many. We met many friends there and mostly just swam and played. Often we rented a cabin for the weekend and did much fishing. Mother caught the most small fish using her drop line, no fishing pole. Once we were going to drive to Lake Michigan for the weekend but had car trouble which used up our money so we came back home.

The World's Fair in Chicago was in 1933, so at eight, this is one of my earliest experiences. I had no interest in Sally Rand, the famous "fan dancer" but I do recall a man-made "mountain" which we could walk up and at the top enter a metal slide to reach the bottom. I was afraid to enter the dark slide so I walked back down. I think my younger sister Nancy slid down just fine, so I was embarrassed, and all these years later remember that. In other trips to Chicago, we saw baseball games, went to the museums and other public educational places. I don't recall going downtown then.

When I was about 12, our folks rented a cabin at Glen Lake,

west of Traverse City, for a whole month. Glen Lake was then billed as one of the most beautiful lakes in the country and the water was pure, it was said. Yet we did get "swimmers itch" and had to race to the druggist to buy lotion, which eased the pain. When the weather was windy, we took the boat to nearby "Fisher Lake" which produced much pan fish. When our dad was there for weekends, he would insist the best fishing was way across the lake, which could get nasty if a storm came up.

Sleeping Bear Dunes was a place we visited often that month. Then it wasn't an official National Park and there were no roads to reach the top. So, near a concession stand, we climbed this steep hill of sand and once at the top we ran down. With the steep incline, we probably ran in leaps of about 10 feet, maybe more. At the bottom we bought a soft drink, rested, and then climbed up again. I think there were "dune buggy" rides then but we never took a ride.

There was a nine-hole golf course then, nestled in the wooded hills, so I think we lost many golf balls. Our folks loved golfing, so we did that quite a bit when our dad was there for weekends.

Another feature of this month at Glen Lake was our introduction to Mackinac Island. I think my brother Bruce was old enough to drive, so we took the trip through Petoskey, on up to Mackinaw City. There was no bridge to the Upper Peninsula, and we took our first ferry boat ride to the island. The coal-burning boat left quite a trail of black smoke, but it was a smooth crossing. Even now I can't get enough of Mackinac Island. This month-long vacation made me fall in love with that part of Michigan.

Coney Island Hot Dogs entered our lives in Kalamazoo at an early age. Not far from the center of town, Main and Burdick, was a seedy eating place that featured these tasty gems. In the window you could see the bowl of secret sauce cooking and if the order was large enough, the old chef-owner placed a metal sheet on his left arm. Then he reached into a cooking oven for the soft moist buns that he placed on the sheet. Quickly he splashed mustard on each hot dog that had been placed in the buns, topped them with plenty of sweet onions and finally ladled the "secret sauce" over the top of each dog. Before he was finished, I was already drooling, but still ordered a soft drink and then went to work on at least two dogs. In later years, the owner was still at it, but with a bit of palsy. He had a hard time keeping a large order on the serving tray nestled on his arm. He finally sold the business, but within the past year,

I could testify that this taste was just as good as ever. In the army, out on maneuvers, eating canned and boxed food, I dreamed of the Kalamazoo Coney Island Dogs.

When I was small, my dad and Uncle Mark Putney would head for the wrestling matches at the Armory. First we had to have a Coney Island or two. Our seats were often on the front row next to the ring, and when bodies were thrown out of the ring near us, I was scared to death. As I listened to the fans shouting, I don't think most of them knew it was all a big fake, as I am sure it was then too, but I didn't know it either.

School work was something to do well, I somehow seemed to know. I don't recall any parental lectures, scolding or rewards and maybe it was just my own pride to try to do better than others, or at least as well as others. So, I guess I did work at studying and when our high school class graduated in January, 1943, Stanton Barnes, Philip Mange and I got top honors. I expect my parents were proud. Western gave me a scholarship which paid for a semester of education. The amount? Would you believe it was for $25?

An elementary school event has stayed in my mind. One day a teacher who I didn't particularly enjoy, accused me of cheating and put me out in the hall in a chair, banished from the room. I never cheated and when I got home I was really in tears. As I think about this, I don't recall that my parents took the teacher to task for his mistake, and I wish they had. Oh well, some people say teachers teach and those who can do things, do things. I have known many talented, nice teachers but I know there have been some bum ones, too.

Schooling meant studying, but also participation in many sports, dating for movies and dances, and much more. I don't recall ever being involved in class politics, although many liked to do that.

What kind of work was there before entering the Service? At the Country Club there were two clay courts, so an early job for me was to groom the courts. That meant dragging the courts, watering and rolling a drum weighted with water to harden the surface. Finally, some white lines were put on the courts using string for direction and a little machine that dropped the white powder. At last the nets were put in place and measured to make certain the height was correct, and we placed a wooden stick at the side of each court. When Kalamazoo College built a new stadium the surface was a type of clay, so I did work there too. Today those courts have a hard surface.

One summer I worked at a nearby green house, next to the West Main Cemetery, very near our home on Prospect. The job was six days a week, from early in the morning to supper time and for weeks I was paid $7.50 a week. Halfway through the summer it was raised to $10. The work was hauling dirt, climbing to the green house tops to paint a white substance on the glass to hold some of the sun light out and many other tasks as ordered. The owner's wife gave us instructions, as he was tipping a few beers, and I don't recall that I did much resting from the job.

Sears Roebuck's manager was a friend of our folks, so Bruce and I both worked weekends and longer when school was out. We both were clerks in the hardware department and had our own cash till. My last job there was to be in charge of the house ware department, so to speak, and that meant mostly working with the advertising department. I don't recall having much to do with ordering inventory nor directing the efforts of anyone else, so I was just selling to customers, and not in charge of much. I think the minimum wage started about then or that is what we were paid.

At eight, I was taught how to swing a golf club by the pro at the Country Club. We also got lessons from Bobby Millar, who was the pro for the several courses the city owned, especially Milham Park. He and his wife, Teen, came to the U.S. from Scotland and they had quite an accent and he was a rough character. Since our dad kept the financial books for the public courses, he became a good friend of the Millars. They lived on the Portage side of the course, and often Bobby would drive his car around the course to make sure play was moving along. The course was in excellent shape and many preferred it over the Country Club. Heavyweight boxing champ Joe Louis trained near Kalamazoo and he enjoyed playing golf. At that time, no black person could play on private courses so he often came to Milham Park and one day I followed him around the course and took some pictures. I never played in a golf tournament prior to military Service.

Tennis was a priority for me and I started that at about eight or so. A close Kalamazoo College friend of my parents was Paul Staake, and he was a good player and was teaching two sons, so that is about when I started too. When I was fifteen, I won a boy's tournament beating the son of an Upjohn Company president. When the son became a college player he was much better than I ever was. In later years, I knew the father well. He was on the board of the American National Bank, and I played some non-competitive friendly games with him and other board members. High school tennis was fun, but when summer arrived I put that aside for other activities, often golf. Of course, the 27 months in the Service provided no opportunity for golf or tennis.

To avoid taking a gym class in high school, in the fall, I was on the cross-country running team and just barely made the team. I would finish the race against another team coming in about 6th or 7th. In a state meet with hundreds in the race, it seemed as though I was passing many runners and being passed by others. I think I came in around 20th. Not great, but not bad.

Winter was basketball time. As a tiny guy, somehow our team played a game at half time of a Kalamazoo College game, and I think the two teams made a basket or two. Church league teams were available for many different age groups and that was fun. The YMCA gym that we played in had a running track above where fans could watch the games. This building was leveled in the 1950's, I think. Then came Junior High basketball and I made that team. Our home games were played in a small floor at the top, the third story of the school building. Not room for many fans there. The city had several junior high schools so we had some good competition. Our building was leveled many years ago too. Mr. Zuidema, our coach, taught me how to holler at poor decisions of the officials. I kind of wish he hadn't done that, but he liked to win and so did I.

In Junior High we played touch football, no equipment and no tackling. Fred Zuidema did a great job of teaching us about the sport and in great detail about the rules of the various sports. I was fortunate for that.

At 125 pounds, my heaviest before entering the Service, I wasn't about to play football. I enjoyed intramural touch games, but I had no desire to bust bodies against the stronger guys. Even though I was short, basketball was a good game for me with speed and quickness and good passing skills and defensive success. I never scored many points and in those days great efforts were made to get the ball in close to the basket to the taller guys. The out court shooting was not a first choice then and those shots were taken using two hands, not the one armed shots of today. Our scores for the whole game were very low.

School Team Defeats Cent

Expects Rigid Restrictions at Specia

Central Stars, Edged Out at Holland, Face Two Games This Week

Central high school's varsity basketball cagers, edged out, 33-30, at Holland, Saturday night, look ahead to two games this week. The boys play at Benton Harbor next Friday and then have a home contest Saturday night against Battle Creek. Central players, while Don Boven remains on the injured list, include, left to right, Don Groggel, Johnny Milroy, Ed. Ward who made 13 points to lead both teams last night, Mel Van Dis, Bob Walker and Ted Bauer.—Gazette photo.

High School basketball team, 1942-43

My brother Bruce and sister Nancy and I never officially joined any church until much later in life. Bruce's first wife, Bobbie McAleer Milroy, was brought up a practicing Roman Catholic, so Bruce joined that faith after they married. Nancy's husband, Wight Reade, never joined a church and he was kind of proud that he had never been baptized. Maybe he changed his mind about that. He died in March, 2010. Nancy died on October 11, 1993, and Bruce April 10, 2013.

Bruce and I were exposed to the Episcopal faith as young boys in the choir. Church league basketball required that a boy went to a church, so I did do Presbyterian Sunday school classes.

Our family group never read the bible together, although our mother probably read it a great deal. We never said "grace" before eating. My father told us many times that on the rare occasions that he had dinner with his mother and step-father, who he disliked, that Mr. Stough would say grace and then, when he knew his message was about to end, Mr. Stough would grab for the best piece of chicken before anyone else could pick up a fork. My brother tells me he saw this happen. I have often got a kick watching people leave church and drive their cars fast in front of others showing no courtesy to others at all, maybe racing to get to a restaurant first, not quite the spirit of Christian treatment of others that they had just heard about in the church they had just left.

There were four movie theaters in Kalamazoo which we enjoyed much. A great percentage of Kalamazoo people were of Dutch descent and participated in church, some as many as three days a week. Many of these folks believed then that playing cards, dancing and going to movies bordered on being sins. Childhood friends of Joyce and mine were children of a reformed church minister, and we learned that the family frequently went to movies in other cities, hoping they would not be discovered there.

The Fuller Theater had a lot of Westerns, cowboys and Indians, and Uncle Mark enjoyed going to those double features too. The Capital Theater was opposite the Kuppie hamburger restaurant that also featured a drink much like today's Wendy's frosty. I was told that the brother of Blackstone the magician worked at the Capital which might explain the secret to one of the tricks. Blackstone performed at the beautiful State Theater, Kalamazoo's biggest and best, and still survives. The theater in many ways reminded me of fancy Chicago theaters and the ceiling appeared to be a sky at night, with a moon and sparkling stars everywhere. Blackstone did his famous trick of taking a handkerchief out of his coat and somehow making it appear that it was alive, moving around in front of him. A ring was placed between the magician and the now living white object to prove there were no wires assisting. He even walked in the audience and I never discovered the secret of this stunt.

Another trick had a stage full of people dressed in animal clothing. Blackstone would put on clothing which looked like some animal, say a bear, and then begin to mix with the other animals. Suddenly, a tiger animal would take his head piece off, and there would be Blackstone with his heavy, flowing all-white hair. Then he would put that head back on and soon, a person with a lion outfit would take his head covering off and again it would now be Blackstone. Well, his brother was a twin, the man who reportedly worked at the Capital Theater, so the answer to this trick seems easy to understand.

Duke Ellington's Band often came to Kalamazoo and put on a long show at the State Theater. I recall sitting up near the front and we thought that some of the dances being performed were risqué, but at our young ages, we were probably misinformed. I think the Michigan Theater showed films that were banned to us.

We took many trips to Detroit, but no further east, not even to Windsor, across the river. Our mother's closest friend, Charlotte Pinckney from Kalamazoo College days, lived in Birmingham, so that was always a destination. The museums, Zoo, baseball games, and other public buildings inspired these trips. North was mostly to see Mackinac Island, with some stops at lakes to do some fishing. Lake Arbutus was often a lake chosen for that.

West, Chicago was as far as we ever traveled. South, the highlight was to get to Logansport, Indiana to be with dad's cousin, Dr. Ballard. Their life style was a bit more opulent than what we were experiencing. They had a lady live with them who served as a maid among other duties. She happened to be colored, as a black person was called then. Parties were a big part of the Ballard's lives including lengthy Sunday morning lawn events. Alcohol was featured. Their house had been a farm house north of town, and had a barn and other buildings they had remodeled. There were several "ice boxes" stocked with soft drinks which we were encouraged to take and that was special. At home, an occasional Coke Cola was brought to our house. Charlie and Nina were a happy, fun couple, with a son Doug who was never in good physical health, but he did marry and there was one granddaughter, spoiled just a bit. These trips usually included a round of golf at their nine-hole Country Club, and always excellent dining was provided.

Since we were in the Depression era, trips to Washington D.C., Florida, New York or the west coast were never considered. I never felt deprived in any way.

The only pet we had was Kippy, a small mixed breed dog given to us by a Jewish friend of my dad, who arrived on a day near the Jewish Holiday, Yom Kippur. This dog liked to chase its tail as well as cars and was often hit but never killed, and died a natural death.

The first house I am aware of was a two story wood house on Burnham Drive, off South Rose Street, about five blocks from Main Street. There was a front porch that we jumped from as though we were parachuting to earth. Our mother would scold us and say "wait until your father comes home." We heard that often when we misbehaved. This was a safe neighborhood with many pleasant neighbors. Since there was a several-stall garage off the end of the drive, no cars were blocking the drive and there was space to play behind and between the houses. Today that garage is gone and several cars are parked between and behind the houses which are not well maintained and the area is not safe now. We played in a field beyond the garages which abutted a Jewish church whose windows we broke playing baseball. With a BB gun, I shot a small bird resting on a wire above and I felt bad about that.

Our schools, kindergarten through high school, were all located in an enlarged block only a few blocks from our house. The grades all shared a common playground although the high school had a track, football field and tennis courts several blocks east of the education buildings. High school basketball was practiced in the four story high school building but all games against other teams were played at Western Michigan College's gym on Oakland Drive, several blocks west of the high school. Kalamazoo College was next to Western so we could walk to any event there. Milham park, with its Zoo, swimming pool, picnic tables and golf course was a long walk, so we rode a bike or were given a car ride there. Our family never owned more than one car, so most everything we attended in town was done by walking.

Kalamazoo has been known as the Celery City, with stalks sold on the streets, and known as the Paper City, due to the many paper mills in the area, the largest being Sutherland Paper Company which employed about 6,000 in Kalamazoo. In the Depression era, Kalamazoo prided itself on being a "debt free" city with a city manager, city commission and mayor form of government. The 1875 national lawsuit which authorized taxing the public to support high school education was the "Kalamazoo law suit."

The Upjohn Company became the strongest part of the Kalamazoo economy, and most capital projects, buildings at Kalamazoo College, additions to both hospitals, senior citizen homes and United Way drives were all successful due to the support of Upjohn Company and its key owners of Upjohn and Gilmores. These same folks supported the civic theater, the symphony orchestra, art center and educational and cultural activities.

The Kalamazoo economy was strong due to many other businesses. The Markin family built Checker Cabs here and the Shakespeare family built fishing rods, and later golf clubs. Atlas Press Company built machines and brother Bruce later was marketing manager for that firm. Heavy metal companies were here too, tied in with the automotive industry. Kalamazoo had a diversified economy. It was a safe place to live and there were no racial problems and blacks were less than five percent of the population.

Western Michigan, Kalamazoo College and Nazareth College were very important to the economy too.

Community concerts brought Jeanette MacDonald, Paul Robeson and many other famous performers. Naturally there were parades, county fairs, and more to entertain the citizens.

A summer highlight was the arrival of more than one circus each year. Trains carrying the animals, tents and people arrived early in the morning so lots of us got up to see the arrival and then watched the tents be installed as the elephants pulled on the ropes and teams of men pounded in the stakes to secure the huge tents. Of course later in the day we returned to see the performance. One night, a friend and I slept in a small tent behind our house and got up early to walk down to the circus grounds which were about ten blocks north of our house. I guess we had no idea what time it really was. A policeman stopped us downtown because it was the middle of the night and he wondered what we were doing, such little guys out like this. He let us go on. Years later, that would have been a very unsafe place for even a strong adult to be, let alone two small boys.

A great influence on my life was Uncle Mark Putney. When he and my mother's sister, Marian, married they first rented an apartment about a half block from where our house was. He and I became buddies, and as I grew up I saw him in all kinds of circumstances. Until they had their children, Lynn and Tim, I was kind of like a son to Mark. He came to watch me participate in sports, he and I played ping pong at his bank, shot baskets and did other things at the YMCA. He liked to sail small boats at Gull Lake and we often played tennis on private courts of his friends. Having graduated from the University of Michigan he was a big fan of the football and basketball teams. He would take me and my father to home games and I watched football star Tom Harmon play. I have been a Michigan fan since then. Mark was not perfect, of course, but when Michigan played poorly he was not a happy camper. Even at a Detroit Tigers game that he took me to, we left early as they were losing, and then were stuck in traffic as we listened on the radio to their come back, and the Tigers won the game.

I used to mow their lawn, clean the garage and do other things, probably for pay. When his bank owned some property at Lake

Michigan, we often spent a day there in some secluded private property. I babysat for Lynn and Tim as Mark and Marian went out of town or on a trip. Mark could tell great stories about people and things he had observed, most quite funny. He never told jokes, and his language was never foul. He was just a very smart, kind man; fun and great to be with. Marian was very special too, a charmer, interested in everything, skilled in drawing art and many more things and loved by everyone. Mark did have a bad habit of sending food back at restaurants, and sometimes being sharp with the wait people. Marian would charm these folks right back. How fortunate I was to be with this couple.

Frank and Helen Leander were other close friends. He was a CPA and manager of the Ernst and Ernst Kalamazoo office. He was a golf buddy of my father, also a billiards friend at the table in the lower level of a local hotel. I often went on fishing trips with them and sometimes I was with Frank alone. Later he became a drinking buddy of my dad, maybe earlier too.

Another interesting couple was Norm and Louise Carver. He was the manager of the local Civic Theater and today there is a nearby building named after him. They both were actors in various plays at the theater. Norm was one of the city's best golfers and dad played with him a lot. They lived on a farm and had us use some of their land to plant a war-time victory garden.

Art Woolam and his wife were close too. Art played golf and the two couples played a lot of bridge. Mark and Marian Putney were at our house on many Sunday nights as the men took on the women in bridge. If the men won they claimed to have a special system named after a contraction of their combined last names, such as "The Putroy" system.

Our folks enjoyed being with many people and all seemed to be kind, interesting and never foul or crude.

What about the birds and the bees? Our mother left a few books around for us to look at and on one walk my father gave me some advice to keep my zipper zipped, whatever that meant. In school a nurse gave a lecture to a class, maybe just boys, and Fred Zuidema was there to observe only. Well at some age, interest in the girls happened. My first kiss was from Patsy one afternoon in her house with several other kids, and the shades pulled, some kind of a game. Then still very young, we had parties at Stanton Barnes' house, encouraged by his mother. "Spin the milk bottle" was a kissing game I recall. Then came Lois that I took to dances and movies, and since my close friend Lee Koopsen dated and married her sister we double dated, some smooching at her house and elsewhere. For my high school prom I took another Jean and got one kiss at the door. Finally I dated Margaret who smooched too, and became my war time pen pal. Entering the service, no girlfriend and I did other than kiss, no touching, no clothes off, no views of secret places; that was it. I never heard of a clitoris or where it was. That was what it was like for many of us, but we probably were in the minority. So much for the birds and the bees. There was no drinking for me or these girls so maybe that kept us inhibited, probably so.

There were three friends in my youth that caught the country's attention: John "Jack" Briley, Louie Spitters and Bruce Thomas. Jack lived around the corner on the next street. He was part of the "kick the can" neighborhood group and one summer he had me out to a cottage at Gull Lake, nothing fancy but a fun week. Suddenly his family moved to Detroit and we lost contact. Then, in January 1943, he and I were freshmen in a Rhetoric class that Miss Master taught with only three other guys in the class that met five days a week for an hour. So, Jack and I got to know each other as young men. Our teacher changed the format of the class to prepare us for our approaching military careers and she was a great teacher. The semester ended and Jack and I went separate ways. I later learned that he enrolled at the University of Michigan and a professor spotted something in Jack and urged him to move on for study in England, which he did. Jack's mother worked in Kalamazoo at the Gilmore department store and she told me a bit that she knew of her son's life.

Then, one night, Joyce and I were watching the Academy Awards program and honors began to pile up for the movie *Gandhi*. Suddenly we were watching Jack give his acceptance speech for writing the movie screen play for *Gandhi* and thus winning that award. I wrote him a congratulatory letter and also wrote Miss Master to let her know that one of the five men in her 1943 class had succeeded. Jack mailed her the screen play. When she wrote me she said "I am a birder, and you live where the Kirtland's Warbler nests, and if you don't know that, you ought to." Sounded like the great teacher she was. Sometime later, Western Michigan arranged an award for Jack and coordinated the showing of *Gandhi* at the State Theater the day after the dinner awards ceremony. He asked the committee to invite me to these functions, so Joyce and I were in Kalamazoo for this.

Saturday afternoon, Max Doolittle, a jeweler, took Jack and me on his small boat at Gull Lake, and pointed out our "rich and famous" folks living on the lake. Then, that evening we were invited to a home on Gull Lake where our hosts, Jack and Joyce and I enjoyed a delicious dinner. We listened to many stories from Jack. He thought he was about to win an award for his screenplay for *Cry Freedom* which was produced by his friend Dickie Attenbourough, who had done *Gandhi* too. The film *Marie,* about a lady who blew the whistle on corrupt politicians in the justice system in Tennessee and starred Sissy Spacek, was quite an experience for Jack. He felt folks were following him as he sought material, and he feared for his life. That was quite an evening.

Louie Spitters was a close friend of Lee Koopsen and had a great looking sister in my homeroom at Kalamazoo Central High School. During the depression days, Louie's mother took in the wash for other families to earn money to help balance the family budget. Louie graduated from The University of Michigan and took a job in a New York brokerage house and soon decided to start his own business. The business was called Memorex and became a well-known manufacturer of tapes for music. Many stories were written about him in business papers and magazines. Then came a day when problems happened in his business and a bank moved him out of the business. Lee Koopsen told me about the big hotel that Louie owned in Hawaii and his palatial California home which the Koopsens visited often. When the Koopsens celebrated their 50th Wedding Anniversary in Kalamazoo, Louie attended along with many other friends. Lee sat me next to Louie so I heard interesting things including his success in getting a single ticket at the NCAA Final Four tournament, without getting scalped, and always a good seat.

Bruce Thomas was the other childhood friend who did great things. He studied at Western and then at The University of Michigan and joined U.S. Steel, first in Duluth, Minnesota. Then he was sent to South America for a few years and finally to the home office in Pittsburgh as his responsibility grew. He finally became the highest ranking financial person in the company. Western Michigan honored him in many ways and he served on various boards at Western. When I moved to Alpena, in a couple of years I was the chairman of the United Way Annual Drive. The year before, Dolly Cole, wife of the CEO of General Motors gave the Kick-off Dinner speech.

I wrote Bruce to see if he would give the speech for our dinner and he accepted. A corporate jet flew him to Alpena, and he came to our house for a pre-dinner drink with a few friends. His previous letters reminded me that he had a bit of a crush on Joyce and her friend Ginny. The next day I drove him to Rogers City where U.S. Steel had a plant. As I watched his easy manner with his staff and others he seemed like the same person I had known and in no way showed signs of being filled with his importance, just a nice guy.

In 1939 or 1940, we moved to 141 S. Prospect, a few blocks northwest of Kalamazoo College and one mile west of Main and Burdick. I think I was told the cost was about $6,000 in those dollars. Across the street was the mansion of the Al Connable family. They had a tennis court next to our street and we were invited to use the court anytime. Our house was stucco, three stories counting a high ceiling attic, with shoots to drop clothing to the basement. The dining room had evidence that buttons could be pushed to call a maid, and there was a side entrance to reach the maid's quarters. The living room was spacious and had a fire place. There were four bedrooms upstairs but only one bath. The location was very upscale from our previous residence. We still had one car, probably company owned, and a single car garage with a driveway shared with our neighbor, Dr. Charles Boys. They had two sons that were university professors. Later, Rolla Anderson and his family were the neighbors. He was football coach and athletic director at Kalamazoo College. This was a great neighborhood to be in the three years before I entered the Service. In 1962, Joyce and I bought the home from my folks as they moved to a smaller house; the price was about $17,000. In 2009 the house was listed for sale at $247,000 and in 2010 it is probably listed lower.

Laughter existed in our house, sometimes listening to radio broadcasts of Jack Benny and Mary Livingston, Fibber McGee and Molly, Fred and Gracie Allen and finally Amos and Andy. The rest of the laughter happened when any one of us made a mistake. When I was small I couldn't say fish, rather "sish" and "Mildred Dame" for Notre Dame. So at the dinner table if someone could trick me to make these mistakes, a huge laugh was generated. I guess our family was taught to be quite judgmental, and critical. No joke jokes were told and the language was always clean, no swearing. Even though I was afraid of my father, I was proud of both parents and how well they mixed with their friends, of whom there were many.

63

My brother Bruce entered service in the Air Force to learn about air plane radios and his first assignment took him to Chicago. He stayed at the Webster Hotel, at Lincoln Park West and he had a great time. In June, 1943, my friend Mel Van Dis and I were invited to sleep at Bruce's place and we had a great time seeing *Goodnight Ladies*, a risqué play for us at the Blackstone Theater.

I was ready to enter the service and I feel that the first 18 years of my life were very fortunate ones for me. During this time, I never had a serious illness, never broke a bone, and never had anything go really wrong. Of course the usual colds, kids' diseases, minimized by vaccinations and other shots were part of life. Visits to doctors' offices, and regular dentist appointments happened. Oh, I did have my tonsils cut out, so the ether smell and the subsequent ice cream treat stayed in my mind.

Had I been raised and trained to be a warrior and defend our country?

I don't really think so. As I have already mentioned, I had never gone hunting, and never handled a gun of any kind. Ready to be an infantryman? Nope. I thought I was headed for military training, then to a college for two years and then the war would be over.

I arrived home in time to enroll at Western, with no idea what to study other than what I thought were challenging classes; things like math, science, foreign languages and some business. Economics, Sociology, English and Psychology were not on my list. A career in engineering or even dentistry was maybe something to consider, but my counselor signed me up for a "General Degree", whatever that meant.

Twenty seven months in the service probably didn't help me mature. Our food, clothing and shelter were provided and we were told what to do. We were not required to make too many decisions other than try to survive when in battle, which was only about seven months of the service time. So, when I returned I stayed at my parent's house, used the GI Bill to cover education costs, and accepted the $20 a week for the first 52 weeks.

I knew I would work to get good grades even though I had no idea how to use the various subjects, and I ultimately did graduate with honors. We had learned to drink beer in the army, but still at only 20 years of age, a bunch of us had to drive to Paw Paw, 15 miles west, to drink at the Village Pump. I usually got sick on the trip back to Kalamazoo, and I hope we had a designated driver. Lois became a fun girl to be with a lot. We got acquainted in the fall of 1946, and parted in 1947. My first summer back I took some summer school classes and I had played on the Western tennis team that spring.

In the summer of 1947, as well as 1948, I was invited to work at the House of Three Bears at Green Lake Wisconsin. The first year I was the maintenance man, which meant making daily driving trips to get groceries and other supplies. Whenever the toilets got plugged, that was my problem to solve, often by just bringing lake water to the offending toilet. We had time off and on a vacation day we either crossed the lake to sip a beer or, during the day, took a canoe a few miles down the lake to Lawsonia, where tennis and golf were available. Mary Delano from Kalamazoo, whose father was a state senator, was on the staff. The camp had a hundred or so boys and girls ages 6 to 10, who were dumped by their wealthy parents for three months, some from as far away as Memphis, Tennessee. The leader of the camp, a lady, visited families in their homes to talk about the camp and, by letter, told the parents how their children were doing. Mary had a boyfriend, Bob Rizzardi, who came up to visit her. I found space in the large tent where a few guys were housed, so Mary, Bob and I became lifelong friends in 1947. That fall we all were enrolled at Western and soon they were a married couple. Bob and I didn't make the Western basketball team, so we entered a city league program, recruiting other Western athletes who couldn't make Western's varsity. We had a great time, even playing games in other cities and Wayne Terwilliger was on our team. The coach, Buck Reade knew he had made a mistake with Wayne, so he made him a starter on the varsity team. Wayne was an outstanding baseball player too and subsequently he played professional ball in the Big Leagues and as a coach, lastly at Minnesota.

Mary's dad had a section of land near Comins, Michigan and he had a retreat house near two lakes, Dollar and Tote Road, filled with large blue gill and bass. One summer, Mary, Bob and I took a trip together starting at this camp. Carl Delano, as a Senator, entertained friends here, and the tables and book cases were filled with mementos given to him. We traveled to the Upper Peninsula headed for Green Lake to see our first meeting place.

In 1947-48, I continued with classes, parties and dates with no one special, but with the Rizzardis often, and that summer I returned to Green Lake, now as a counselor. I had four ten-year-old boys in a hut for three months. Each week the head of the camp would meet with each counselor to discuss what progress had been made with the boys and girls and what new plans we had to help the kids along. This summer, I had a great girlfriend. She was in college and her first name was Seena, and she was very Italian. We stayed pen pals after the camp and the following spring she traveled from Chicago by train to attend a dance at Western. When we had left camp in August 1948, I rented a hotel room on the north side of Chicago. We met for dinner and then I returned her back to her north-side home. I waited on the street for a bus to take me to the hotel. I wasn't worried about safety but I bet a few years later that would have been dangerous.

Each spring the Tennis Team took spring trips and then our conference season began. When we played at Northwestern, our Three Bears camp leader was there to watch me play; I lost. I earned five letters on the team and the last year I was the best player and was named captain. I had to play the best player on all the other teams and was just not that good. Maybe I won one match that season. I was ready for golf.

Coach Kim Peterson entered his second year as tennis coach at Western facing a tough schedule of eleven meets and two conference tournaments. The squad this year boasts five returning lettermen who are being pushed by several new candidates for varsity berths. The five veteran netmen include John Milroy of Kalamazoo, Jim Jankowski and John Lychuk of Detroit, Don Constant of Grand Haven, and Ray Postema of Muskegon. The loss of Arnie Brown by graduation was felt considerably, as Arnie was number one singles man last year and teamed with Milroy helped to make up the top doubles combination.

John Milroy is the only senior on the squad, while Jankowski, Postema, and Lychuk are juniors and Constant is a sophomore. Among the candidates from whom Coach Peterson hopes to draw some varsity material are John Bailey from Battle Creek, Bill Sagin of Detroit, Norm Deiters of Muskegon Heights, John Kellogg of Battle Creek, Dave Kistler of Kalamazoo, and Ivan Elovitch of Gary, Indiana.

1949 TENNIS SCHEDULE

April 19—Vanderbilt at Nashville

April 20—Southwestern at Memphis

April 21—Alabama at Tuscaloosa

April 22—Mississippi at University

April 29—Wayne at Kalamazoo

April 30—Cincinnati at Kalamazoo

May 5—Notre Dame at South Bend

May 11—Michigan State at Kalamazoo

May 12—Northwestern at Kalamazoo

May 21—Michigan State at East Lansing

May 27, 28—Mid-American Conference
at Kalamazoo

June 2, 3, 4—Central Collegiate
Conference at Kalamazoo

John Milroy, singles veteran and senior member of the 1949 tennis squad.

1949 TENNIS

Graduating in 1949, I interviewed at Ernst and Ernst in the Chicago office, prearranged by my folks' friend, Frank Leander. I had not majored in accounting, so no luck there. Then a neighbor, manager of Consumers Power in Kalamazoo, set up an appointment in Jackson, Michigan. No luck there either. Uncle Mark Putney could not hire me at the First National Bank, (nepotism policies) but he called a friend at the neighboring American National and I was hired, first in the auditing department. For four years more I lived with my parents on Prospect Street. That was not a good idea. At this point my dad really had a problem with his drinking and he began to lose one job after another and the home atmosphere was not pleasant.

Then in the fall of 1952, Joyce and I started dating. We knew of each other but we were not in school together, the younger lady that she was. I first asked her to join me with Dick Walsh and his Western girlfriend to attend a University of Michigan football game, returning by way of the great Schuler's Restaurant in Marshall, Michigan. The next day we all played tennis, but Dick's friend was an athletic major at Western and she was too talented for us. I had fun, but I'm not sure about Joyce. The following spring I asked Joyce to be my wife and she had to think about that for a time, but finally said yes. She suggested that September would be the best time to marry, not June as I had offered, so September 12, 1953, we tied the knot at St. Luke's Episcopal Church in Kalamazoo, with Charles Bennison the priest performing the service. He later became the Bishop for the Western Michigan Diocese. We joined that church the following year after taking lessons from Fr. Bennison.

Our Honeymoon started in Ft. Wayne, Indiana as we were headed for Gatlinburg, Tennessee. In Gatlinburg we anchored at the Greystone Hotel and at that time there were hardly any motels in this beautiful area. The bears were plentiful as we drove the mountains and cars were few. We have been back many times, always glad to do that, but it is so busy now.

As we headed home we stopped in Columbus, Ohio and there just happened to be a football game, and I am sure Joyce wanted to see the game. Woody Hayes was coaching and "Hopalong Cassidy" was the star who later was a starter for the Detroit Lions

Back in Kalamazoo, we went to our upstairs apartment on Gull Road, renting from a nice Hungarian couple. We moved next to Montrose Street at the hill top of South Westnedge. Jan arrived on

July 16th, 1954. It wasn't long until Mike joined us on November 29, 1955. Then, Tim enlarged the family on October 13, 1958. Picking up the rear was James on June 21, 1960.

Today, Jan is in Des Moines, Iowa. Mike married Kathy Clark on May 15, 1982, and Casey was born August 28, 1988. Brianne was born April 17, 1993. Tim and Vicki married on May 29, 1999, and Andrew was born February 8, 2002. Elizabeth was born March 5, 2004. James and Lori were married on April 27, 1985. Erin was their first born on August 20, 1988, followed by Ellen on April 19, 1991.

Wedding on Sept. 12, 1953, St. Luke's Church Kalamazoo

Richard and Lucille Petersen with Norda and Robert Milroy

Trip to Pike's Peak in 1971

Picture of "kids" in 1972

Big grandma & sister,
below mother Norda
in 1980 & kids

Roots in Delphi, Indiana

Taken in & near Delphi 10/13/00

Since my late twenties I have known that this is God's world and I believe that God can do anything that He or She wants to do. I know that God has ordered things so that action on our part will cause certain reactions God has arranged. We were given the right to think and therefore make whatever decisions we decide to make. God created a world that may have tornados, hurricanes, earth quakes, floods and other tragedies as well as painful illness and I do not understand that.

I have already reported that belonging to an official church is not something that happened to me and my siblings, although I think we were all baptized. Joyce and her two brothers didn't join a church either, maybe neither of her parents did. Her mother did attend St. Luke's, especially if either of her sons was participating in the Boy's Choir. When I entered the Army I was given a small New Testament Bible by the Presbyterians since mother was an active member there, and I still have it.

In the service, while I was often scared to death, I don't think I prayed for God's help ever. All of my army Catholic buddies were pretty faithful about going to church, and they probably prayed to God.

So, when I was 28, Joyce and I joined St. Luke's Episcopal Church in Kalamazoo, Michigan and the priest was still Fr. Charles E. Bennison, the same man who married us. He was a charismatic, freshly scrubbed, cherubic man who exuded love and was a super salesman. At Diocesan conventions, with hundreds present, he could call most by their first names. He always had an agenda and our first opportunity to pledge to a capital campaign was for money to tear down the old majestic parish hall to have a modern, efficient new building with space for offices, guild rooms, many class rooms and rooms for vestry meetings and for choir practice. Pledging to that and to an operating budget was new for us.

Early in my Episcopal career I was asked to attend a weekend meeting at the Diocese retreat house near Holland, Michigan, very near Lake Michigan and its beautiful sandy beach. There was a group of about twenty, both lay people and priests, to listen to a man from an eastern U.S. Diocese. His mission was to teach us about the history of, and the need to do, tithing.

From late Friday afternoon through Sunday afternoon, we mixed learning, eating, having communion services and socializing. Looking back, I was really brain washed, falling for the message intellectually and emotionally, and I am glad that it happened. Our family began to tithe, not modified by tax considerations or our other giving, and we did 10%. I think that kept me closer to the church than had we not done that. Recently, we have done the modern tithe, which means 5%. And through these 55 years of Episcopalian membership we have fallen by the wayside more than once when the leadership did things that seemed out of order to me. That has just happened again in late 2009. The current priest decided to void his "contract" and has moved out of the Rectory, which sits empty months later.

Staying close to the church, in Kalamazoo, Ft. Dodge, Iowa and finally here in Alpena, Michigan, in good times and in stressful times has helped my life I am sure. We have learned to know many fine church folks, and I have participated in many interesting projects, Diocesan meetings and much more. My most important male role model was Uncle Mark Putney and I am very aware that he lived an honorable and kind life but had nothing to do with the institutional church. I also have known too many church leaders, both lay and clergy, who have almost driven me from the church.

Father Bennison's next project was to open a new parish in Portage, Michigan, called St. Barnabas. With that behind him he opened St. Martin's on the west side of Kalamazoo. His last new parish was near Gull Lake, Michigan and I was present for the ground breaking. Then it became time for him to seek the office of Bishop for the Western Michigan Diocese. I am quite sure that old "barleycorn" got the best of the Bishop who placed his hands on Joyce's and my head to officially bring us into the church. I had enjoyed his melodic, low-ranged voice but I think maybe the heavy imbibing helped bring about some of that sound.

Fr. Bennison competed for the Bishop job against the priest who led the parish in the Grand Rapids church which housed the Bishop's Chair. Once elected, Bennison persuaded the Diocese that the better location for the Cathedral was near Kalamazoo, which really did not make much sense other than to get him away from political problems with the Grand Rapids Priest that he had defeated. Bennison had some very wealthy folks of the Kalamazoo area in his camp, so he set about building a new Cathedral that looked like an English Castle, and offered a circle in the round communion area. The $1.7 million project was completed and in the process he held special meetings with the more affluent members of St. Luke's and their sycophants to invite them to become members of the new Cathedral congregation. Many did so, if not most.

St. Luke's hired Fr. James C. Holt to replace Bennison and he was a very different man in appearance and in style - maybe more principled and less pragmatic than Bennison. The new Bishop expected St. Luke's to pledge to the new Cathedral, even though he had taken many families with money with him. St. Luke's raised the money and never did Fr. Holt object to any of these events and he turned out to be an excellent leader. His pastoral care was exceptional and his Yale education was apparent. He could say more in a five-minute homily than most priests I have heard over the years could do with a half hour.

Fr. Holt led a growing parish; got things done that needed to be done and did it by dropping ideas to be picked up by the layman and women rather than by ordering things which was Bennison's style. To celebrate the first ten years of Fr. Holt's residency a memo was sent to the members suggesting that we all participate in a fund-raiser to send our priest's family on a vacation. No follow-up memos were sent and no telephone calls made, but a substantial sum was raised with close to 100 percent participation and this came as a surprise to the Holts.

When we moved to Ft. Dodge, Iowa, we found a very unusual situation at small St. Mark's Church. A doctor had set up two trusts with two local banks so that at his death income from the one trust would be sent to St. Mark's Church, and a similar amount would be used to care for his wife. At her death all income would then go to the church. Only, she predeceased him by a day, so all the income went to the church. The layman leaders decided to do many capital expenditures and borrowed money from the banks for this to be repaid from the trust income. No living church members needed to give a penny to the new building project. When we arrived, there were about 43 pledges to the operating budget. I found too many of the parishioners were unhappy with their rather old priest, wanting him to retire. I enjoyed him and learned to know him fairly well when I was elected senior warden of the vestry.

I thought it would be a good idea if we could get the court to let the church invade the trusts to get funds to liquidate the debt.

Then there would still be substantial income coming from the remaining trust balances, which could be used for new projects such as scholarships for nurses or whatever. At least the church could be working on some new, positive matters rather than being obsessed with the unhappiness with the priest. Some other key members on the vestry agreed with this concept. Soon, the Iowa Bishop made a call on the church and its vestry and he heard a lot of complaining. As I listened to this, for the only time in my life, I felt that I needed to speak up and with no preparation. God would help me through; somewhere I had heard that idea. I told the Bishop the concept some of us had and his reaction was "go for it." So, we formed a committee and a talented marketing man in a branch of a large company led the way. He prepared visual aids and as senior warden it was my job to present this to a parish meeting. We called the meeting and were supported with no opposition that I recall. It was taken to the court, but denied, I was told, since at that time I was in Alpena.

One other fun experience in Ft. Dodge was when the plush, red center-isle carpet began to curl up so that we were concerned that members might trip on it. What to do? Ideas to take all the pews out and stretch the carpet or put in new carpet and other ideas came up. Then we learned about a man who had a talent to solve this problem. For about $50 he would perform his magic. He planned to come into the church on a warm, spring Friday night and turn the heat way up in the church and pour water on the carpet everywhere. Then, a day later, the heat would be turned off and the carpet would be as flat as new. Whether this would work or not, or whether the red carpet would be stained, no one knew. We decided to go ahead, and the weekend was Palm Sunday with attendance expected to be high. I crossed my fingers, and lo and behold, it worked. I had known about men who had a talent with a stick to search for water, a "divining rod" it was called, I think. We had a similar man, only he was taking the water away, so he was a "reverse divining rod" man.

In Alpena almost 35 years, I have been on the vestry, senior warden at least once, deeply involved in two successful $100,000 capital campaigns, on a Diocese committee and have attended a few conventions. We have had five priests over this time. A few years ago at a convention, a young priest from Jackson, Michigan, was there to make speeches about his leadership of young people. He was being aggressive that his choice was to be a practicing "gay" priest. Now we have the same thing, only the men are Bishops. This, and other less-than-conservative policies, is causing many problems in the church in the United States.

Many years ago the Michigan Bishop decided to take on the priest of the Mariner's Church in downtown Detroit. This priest was a conservative person who would not lead his flock in the new ways. The Bishop tried to take the church building away as he tried to banish the priest from this parish.

Hundreds of thousands of dollars of legal expense to the Diocese resulted in the court refusing to give the Bishop the building. The same thing is happening in Pennsylvania today, as Bishop Bennison, son of the man who married us, is trying to defrock a priest and keep his building for the Diocese. I think this Bishop has been booted out for other reasons, connected with his brother who had done improper things, known by the Bishop. That brother, John, left the priesthood several years ago in San Francisco, California.

The Kalamazoo Cathedral of Bennison is out of existence now. The Cathedral Congregation could not afford the costs and the Diocese refused to set up an endowment for that purpose. Today the property has been sold and the buyers are constructing a larger building near the ex-Cathedral. The new occupant is of a fundamentalist faith, I believe, and very busy I hear.

About twelve years ago, the northeast part of Michigan, where Alpena is located, decided, for some reason, that it would be best to form a new Eastern Michigan Diocese. A Bishop has come and gone after ten years and there is a new Bishop. I was very disappointed that the new Diocese was formed. I do not believe that anyone could prove that the new Diocese has improved anything in the 60 or so churches and missions under the new jurisdiction. We are no longer part of a mix of races as before.

While I have been in the Alpena church 35 years, I learned a few years ago that I am way out of step with the others belonging to this church. Lately, I have avoided being on the vestry, but was asked by the newest priest to be on a new finance committee, so I said yes. About three years ago, the vestry made a list of many capital projects and a drive was started to raise money to purchase a new organ console, estimated at $55,000. The list included a new church roof, major work at the rectory and other projects, added up to over $200,000 for the needs. The Rector went to a bank and secured approval for a loan of this amount, he reported. As a member of the finance committee, I was surprised at his action. With no consultation with the committee, maybe he already had vestry approval and felt consulting with his finance committee was unnecessary. In hindsight, I wish the committee had been dissolved. I thought up a plan to sell the rectory for several reasons and I ran the idea by a few, who concurred. Then I took it to the finance committee and the group approved the plan. It was suggested that it be taken to the vestry, which I did. There was only one dissenting vote on the vestry and I was asked to present the idea to a special parish meeting. I did my best, but the only comments were from fine folks who thought the idea was a bad one. Not one voice from either the finance committee or the vestry was expressed in support, and one vestry man changed his mind and now was against the idea. While there was a temporary postponement of the vote until the Annual Meeting, it was clear that the idea failed in great numbers. Now a few years later, the rectory would probably sell for half of the value when the idea was first presented. However, I would take odds that at a future date, the rectory will have to be sold, just as the Kalamazoo Cathedral had to be sold, and as reported earlier, the current priest has vacated the rectory.

I have been told that a former priest told his son-in-law that half the people in the business are actors ahead of their responsibility and capability to deliver God's Word. Who knows if that is true, but I have witnessed a few that I felt enjoyed being performers more than anything, even to the point that they thought they had a mission to make everyone laugh in church. The Episcopal Church is not very large in numbers in the U.S. and there are no reports of rapid growth. The huge churches seem to be the ones that stick to a conservative position, and comedy isn't part of it.

Once I may have read a version of the bible all the way through, old and new testaments. I am sure I did some skimming. As I read, I decided that God must have quite a sense of humor as He, over and over, gives man a new chance to correct things, and man just keeps right on failing. I think I have a feel for what the spirit of the New Testament is and if I follow that, I will not make too many mistakes. However, I have no confidence in the literal words that *man* wrote in the bible, not God. Church leaders have just been people who can be filled with greed, desire for power and fame rather than love, just as people are today. So when words come from the pulpit proclaiming what Christ was thinking or saying, my mind thinks, here is another actor.

Joyce and I had our family exposed to the church as they grew up, and I am glad about that. As adults, they will decide what they want to do about any church and that is as it should be. In Kalamazoo, St. Luke's decided to place a mission near the growing campus of Western Michigan University. The day that President Kennedy was assassinated, November 22, 1963, I completed the agreement for the purchase of the property where St. Aiden's would be located. A successful fund-raising campaign was held, architects engaged and construction started. Every Sunday I would take all four of our children from church to watch the week's progress. At completion we had a small chapel, accommodations for a priest with an office, social area with a fireplace and in the lower level a kitchen and room for gatherings, including musical performances of that era. An inexpensive noon-day soup kitchen was offered and ROTC and Vietnam protesters often ate side by side. This was a great project offered under Fr. Holt's leadership.

Once, we were on the campus of Harvard University and there I bought books of Peter J. Gomes, a highly regarded Baptist Minister. However, in 2010 in a new book of Tony Horwitz, I read a response Gomes gave to Horwitz's question; ". . . we should honor myth rather than fact?"

"Precisely," said Gomes. "Myth is more important than history. History is arbitrary, a collection of facts. Myth we chose, we create, we perpetuate... it's like religion, beyond facts Myth trumps fact, always does, always has, always will." One active adulterous priest in the pulpit drove a friend of mine out of the church and I expect the "style" of other priests have turned members away, maybe the actor/comic ones or even the myth pastors. Who knows what really drives a person out of the church?

I have been with an Episcopal Church friend frequently and have heard him say so often, "I wish I could worship God the way my Quaker childhood friend does." He meets with a group various places, preferably outside with nature, weather permitting. His group owns no building, has no minister or staff, no organ or choir, they just meet and meditate together. My friend never mentions if a collection plate is passed around. Neither does he mention that the Quaker faith is what partially molded the character of our ex-President, Richard M. Nixon. Quakers may not be perfect either.

I still attend church on Sundays and Joyce and I offer some financial support to the parish, nowhere near what we have done in the past. As I have clearly reported, I am way out of step with the church membership in Alpena when it comes to financial matters.

Jan is now a member of a Congregational Church in Des Moines, Iowa, and is very involved with activities there and enjoying that. While living in Iowa, she was first attending an Episcopal Church but stopped. Later she joined a fundamentalist group and enjoyed it for a while, but stopped. Now she enjoys her new connection a great deal.

James has been very involved with a Lutheran Church and both of their daughters have received all their education, from kindergarten through high school, in a Lutheran Parochial school system. Lori has been close to the Lutheran Church for many years and has a brother who became a Lutheran minister. James joined the Lutheran Church several years after their marriage.

Tim and Vicki are back in church with their eight and six-year-old children. She grew up in, and attended Parochial Reformed churches and schools. Mike and Kathy and their two daughters have no church involvement. Kathy was brought up a Roman Catholic but left early in her life.

When it comes, my time to depart this world, my wish is that my ashes be placed at the National Cemetery in Ft. Custer, Michigan, near Battle Creek; the place where I entered the Service in 1943. A memorial service can be held at any convenient time, anywhere. Weather may have a lot to do with selecting where and when. There is no need for an Episcopal service.

Kalamazoo close friends, Rizzardis, Griffiths, and Crooks

Kalamazoo St. Luke's

EPISCOPAL CHURCHES

Ft. Dodge St. Mark's

Alpena Trinity

The Bishop's
Service Cross
Award

JOHN ROBERT MILROY

IN RECOGNITION of your faithfulness, devotion and service to the Church, it is my pleasure and privilege to present you with the Bishop's Service Cross.

WITH the presentation of this award are given the congratulations and esteem of your fellow Churchmen throughout the diocese, and my own affection and blessing.

Faithfully yours in Christ,

+ Charles E. Bennison

The Bishop of Western Michigan

anno Domini

1971

Mark Putney married my mother's sister, Marian Schoonmaker, in Kalamazoo in 1935. Both became highly regarded in Kalamazoo and rooms were named for each in public buildings. At the Kalamazoo Institute of Arts, a room was dedicated to Marian, and at a Business Center at Western Michigan University, a room was dedicated to Mark.

When I was 10, Mark and Marian lived in an apartment that was only a half block away from Burnham Drive, where our family lived. Mark became a second father for me and a role model, inspiration, mentor and a friend for life. Marian and Mark were busy, talented, kind and fun to be with. They were, above all, principled persons. They had a daughter, Lynn, and then a son, Tim.

When my aunt and uncle traveled, I was asked to "baby-sit," but that was when their children were older. I played games with Tim and when he was the football quarterback in high school I would attend his games. Both Lynn and Tim graduated from the University of Michigan, and when bank meetings were held in Ann Arbor, they would often join us for dinner. Together we would enjoy the speeches and program, which usually was the Michigan Men's Glee Club singing.

The Putneys, in their early married life, moved to many different homes; some in Kalamazoo and some out on farm property. They finally settled in a small farm house with a big barn and chicken house which had not been well maintained during the Depression days. The land was a quarter of a mile east of fashionable Gull Lake, where wealthy folks from Kalamazoo and Battle Creek had summer homes. The Putney property was adjacent to property of wealthy Upjohn Company owners and others. These people became great friends of Marian and Mark and some, business associates of Mark.

Mark graduated from Kalamazoo Central High School and then the University of Michigan, working his way through school, sometimes as a short-order cook. After graduation he joined the First National Bank and Trust Company of Kalamazoo as a teller. This bank was the most prominent of the four Kalamazoo banks, the oldest national bank in Michigan. It did not close permanently during the Depression, as most banks did. It was a sound bank.

Years later, as I worked in the American National Bank and

was given a new desk assignment, I found a loan application of the Putneys' that should have been destroyed. As I looked at it I could see that they actually had a deficit net worth then and not many assets, so I learned that Mark had started his business career from scratch.

Marian had great artistic talents and she had obtained some of her college education in California. She became a teacher in Kalamazoo before they married. She was the leader in making their new rustic house into a very attractive small home for the family of four. Later, as Mark advanced in his banking role, they built a new building to house three vehicles, with other rooms where Mark could bring his friends for card games and other male retreat activities. Later, when family visited, Mark could escape to "his" building to make room for the grandchildren and others. Mark ultimately became President, CEO and Chairman of the bank, and retired when he turned 65.

Mark enjoyed an exceptional banking career. I believe his objectives were to manage a sound, safe and profitable bank and to develop and train a staff prepared to manage the bank at his retirement, and he did that. He also had an objective to have a good time, in and out of the bank, to be a sound banker, but to have fun doing that. He had no desire to gain prominence or attention in a public way. He did not try to become President of the Michigan Banker's Association or gain national titles. The men who followed him did seek such honors and some succeeded in that quest. He was an excellent lender and supported Robert Morris Associate's activities. That organization was important to bank lenders, nationally.

As I think about Mark's career, it is clear that he was a leader as banking changed during the time he was at the helm.

I learned in time that many influential and affluent families looked to Mark for counsel in their financial matters. These people trusted him completely, and respected him for his intelligence, education and experience. I learned about integrity from him, more than from anyone else.

I believe Mark started a Kalamazoo banking tradition in how to honor a new bank president in one of the local banks. A time was set to organize a parade of the other bank presidents and several of their top assistants. All wore top hats as they marched down the main street, while they carried a huge sympathy wreath that would normally be placed at a funeral parlor. The local policeman, stationed

master charge
THE INTERBANK CARD

INTERBANK

In May, most of the American National Bank American Security Charge Cardholders were mailed their new Master Charge Credit Card. At the time of mailing, it was reported that over 2,100 banks with 4500 banking offices throughout the United States were issuing these cards. This provides opportunities to charge at over 300,000 stores, professional offices and service establishments.

Master Charge is a member of the Interbank Card Association. Through this affiliation Master Charge cardholders can use their cards in all fifty states and in ten foreign countries.

Many observers of the fast-changing bank credit card scene anticipate that ultimately most banks will be either part of the Master Charge-Interbank Card Association, or the BankAmericard program, initiated by the Bank of America. This step definitely keeps The American National in tune with the rapidly changing credit card field.

A NEW PRESIDENT

Tradition in Kalamazoo was followed in June as present and former bank presidents paid their respects (condolences) to the newest member of the fraternity — James H. Duncan, new President of The First National Bank and Trust Company.

Marching down the street with the traditional wreath are, Ray Allen (former President of Home State Bank of Lawrence, Bob Rogge (Past President of the First State Bank of Mendon), Francil Hamilton (Past President of Industrial State Bank — now with the First National), Harold Jacobson, our President, Charles Finley (in spite of his size, hidden — Past President of Industrial State Bank), Mark Putney (First National's Chairman of the Board), and Garret Van Haaften, our Chairman of the Board.

OUTSIDE JIM'S OFFICE - SMILES

GET ACQUAINTED WITH ATHENS

John Butler   Betty, Delores, and Lonn

Athens is a community of approximately 1,000 people. located eighteen miles south of Battle Creek on M-78. Athens is in the southwest corner of Calhoun County and by road is the most distant office from our Downtown Kalamazoo Office.

The manager of our Athens Office is John R. Butler. John joined the former First State Bank of Mendon in March, 1966. Prior to that he had worked for the Bank of Lenawee County in Adrian for sixteen years. John was a native of Adrian. He is a 1958 graduate of the School of Banking and the University of Michigan and a 1963 graduate of the School of Consumer Banking at the University of Virginia. John has also received his pre-standard and standard certificates through the A.I.B. In Athens John is past president of the Rotary Club and sings in the choir of The Congregational Church. John and his wife have two children, a boy and a girl.

Assisting John at the Athens Office is Lonn B. Spencer. Lonn is 22 years old and graduated from the Athens High School in 1965. While attending Michigan State University, he gained valuable banking experience by working part-time for the Bank of Lansing. Lonn joined The American National in July, 1968. Lonn has furthered his education by taking many A.I.B. courses. Lonn and his wife are the proud parents of a 7-month old boy.

The head teller at the Athens Office is Betty Wank. Betty is a native of Athens and graduated from Athens High School. She joined the bank in August, 1964. Betty's husband is employed at General Foods in Battle Creek and they have two children, a boy, seventeen and a girl fourteen. In Athens Betty has been very active in the Band Boosters and currently serves as its Treasurer.

You may remember Delores Hayes, since she was the one who won the television set in our American Security Charge Card Contest. Delores and her husband moved to Athens two years ago following her husband's retirement from the Detroit Police Force after twenty-five years of service. As a girl, Delores lived in Athens during the senior year of high school and she and her husband liked Athens so well that they decided to get away from the big city and come here for retirement. Delores and her husband have two girls, one is married and the other lives at home. They also have one grandson. Her interests are playing bridge, bowling and winning television sets.

at the main city intersection to guide traffic, pulled out his whistle and stopped all car traffic so that the parade could pass by. The destination was the office inside the bank of the new bank president. When there, speeches were made including that of the new president and of course pictures were taken and publicity given to the local, state and national media sources. Often much was published. This tradition ended when banking became more competitive in the 60's; more serious and not as much fun, I think.

Mark's best friend, president of a competing bank, was a strong competitor, but they did have fun tricking each other. Due to the Depression, the Federal government set many new controlling rules and restrictions. Limits on interest rates on deposits and loans were set and house mortgages were required to have short maturities as well as greater investment by the buyers than later became the rule. Investments were to be in U.S. Government bonds or highly rated municipal securities. Banks could not invest in the stock market and loans for that purpose were tightly controlled. Thus, bank competition was restricted and I think provided the time for fun and shorter banking hours.

Annually in June, the Michigan Bankers' Association held a several-day convention on Mackinac Island. One year Mark arranged to have a horse-drawn hearse placed on the water pier where boats arrived loaded with bank attendees and their wives. Many were alerted to be there before Mark's friend Chuck Finley was to arrive. When he did, he was made to lie in the hearse and was driven to the Grand Hotel. Others were positioned there to greet him. Aunt Marian told me that they also held "pissnics" during the day when the serious bankers were in meetings listening to reports and trying to get elected to important positions. The ladies decorated horse-drawn vehicles with bright flowers and ribbons and they found beautiful spots to spread the lunches where they could eat and drink looking at the blue waters of Lake Michigan and Lake Huron. They had fun.

As a hobby, Mark liked to raise chickens and then give eggs to friends and customers. He also enjoyed growing sweet corn which was the feature for the summer dinners outside their house for friends and customers. The Putneys enjoyed entertaining and when the weather was bad, they went to the Gull Lake Country Club or in Kalamazoo to other nice places.

With their nest finally empty, Marian decided to open a gift store which in time blossomed to several locations. Her stores were next to the Gull Harbor Inn at Gull Lake, another at Diamond Harbor Inn near South Bend, Indiana. Then she opened another at the Whitcomb Hotel, in St. Joseph, Michigan, a spot where many Chicago folks came to stay. In the end she consolidated to one store near the First National, a new large branch located a mile or so south of the main office.

For vacations, Mark and Marian did unusual things such as boarding a banana boat which sailed near South America, or a commercial ship sailing in the Mediterranean Ocean. That trip influenced their decision to open a restaurant on the island of Crete. Retired, and with Marian's business sold, they acquired an old building which had been a small hotel on an inlet to Crete. They had the building remodeled, acquired staff, bought locally made earthen wear pottery and opened for business. For fun, they named various dishes after Kalamazoo friends and the restaurant menu displayed that. Often these friends came to Crete to see them, especially during the colorful religious holiday season. The Putneys owned this for a few years and spent their winters there.

Under Mark's leadership, the bank acquired nearby small, profitable banks and made them part of a branching system. Michigan law at the time prevented banks from putting branches farther than 25 miles from the home office and they could not establish a branch if there already was a bank or branch of a bank in a city. The First National Bank market expanded well and profitably. In Kalamazoo, the other banks, including the one where I was employed, decided to open several "service" branches. Mark opened nothing except a large branch to house a new computer system. The other banks' "service" branches were not profitable, mostly extra cost centers.

Then, the bank regulators told Mark that he should open Kalamazoo branches to better serve his bank's customers who were moving to the town suburbs. The regulators made some threats if he did not conform. To accommodate them, he sent his key man, Jim Duncan, to survey the Kalamazoo market by airplane. About ten congested areas were selected this way, and in a short time, small branch buildings of the same design and color were constructed and opened in these areas. Some of these offices are still open, but the others were closed as the bank easily proved to the regulators that these branches were not profitable for the bank.

Then came the credit card business explosion. A Long Island

bank was the first commercial bank to offer this service, The Franklin National, I believe. This bank was innovative with drive-up banking and other new services. Mark sent Jim Duncan out to learn about this credit card service, and with this knowledge, First National decided to create the service for the South Western Michigan market. This was a great undertaking, and Duncan was selected to lead this. A new staff was trained, a separate location found and equipment and supplies acquired. Service hours were to be 24 hours, since customers could use their new credit card anytime. What a marketing job to convince larger businesses, department stores and others to give up their own credit business to the bank. Small retail businesses that had no service other than cash, could now offer credit to their customers. Jim Duncan led this successfully and became an excellent manager, something that might not have happened so early in his life had he followed the career path of banking at that time.

The other Kalamazoo banks didn't know what to do and incorrectly decided to delay offering the service of credit cards. It was not long before a bank in Battle Creek began to offer the service and The American National where I worked, became part of that plan. Soon hundreds of different plans were offered around the country and then they began to merge. Today, there are basically two plans - Visa and Master Card, and the world is better for that.

Mark's next plans had to do with the expected holding company legislation. Prior to that, banks were restricted in their expansion to broader markets. No branch could be placed further than 25 miles from the bank's home office, and if a town already had a bank or a branch of a bank, no other bank could enter that market. Somehow, there was special legislation for the Michigan National system and State Senator Hooper's gunshot slaying may have had something to do with that ("Three Bullets Sealed his Lips", another story).

Mark asked Jim Duncan to move to a small farming town south of Kalamazoo to broaden his bank training and to learn what presidents of small banks were concerned with. My aunt told me that some of Jim's peers thought he had been demoted, but not so, of course. Prior to this move, Duncan's banking forte had been small loan credit and the related credit card service. Duncan started his career at another local bank and he had not graduated from Western Michigan University who, many years later, honored him as a distinguished graduate. Commercial lending, bank operations, investments and other matters would be new to Jim. He did broaden his education at a special banking school at Wisconsin and he also attended the Northwestern Chicago Campus School on Public Relations. Both of those programs were short summer activities with written reports due in the year.

With the Banking Company legislation passed, the First National of Kalamazoo began acquiring banks located all over the state, including the Upper Peninsula banks. The large Detroit banks began their expansion in southeast Michigan and only many years later reached out to places such as Alpena, Michigan.

Mark's management style in developing his staff included letting them make mistakes, which he expected during their training. Naturally, they couldn't make the same type of mistake too often, but they were not severely reprimanded or fired with the first one. Mark did not tolerate managers making policy changes which he first learned about from customers. He wanted no such surprises. Any insubordination, any unethical behavior or any immoral behavior was not tolerated by Mark, and those activities usually called for dismissal from the bank.

Mark's career was about to end. He had been a leader in building a profitable branching system. He was a leader in being the second bank to offer a credit card service. He led Michigan in covering the state with a branching system under the new holding company legislation. Above all, he had developed a trained staff capable of managing the bank as he retired. No new leaders were brought in from outside the bank, which is what happened in the other Kalamazoo banks.

Mark's last decision was to rent office space in Kalamazoo away from the bank where he could read and study business and personal matters. This gave Jim Duncan the space to manage the bank, with no implied influence from Mark. It may not have been the case had Mark kept an office in the bank. Jim was a smart man and I am sure that he called on Mark often away from the bank seeking his counsel and kept Mark informed. These men stayed friends for life and Duncan often told the world that any success he may have had was due to Mark Putney.

When Mark died, he left ample funds for Marian to enjoy her last years, which included much travel, some with my sister, Nancy, as they traveled down the Amazon River and went to Russia together. The last time I saw Marian to take her to lunch, she was in her 90's, was not seeing well, but still held her upbeat attitude about the world and her life.

My life was made so much better than it ever would have been had I not known Marian and Mark as my close friends and inspiration for good things.

_1984_

Services set Sunday for banker Mark B. Putney

Memorial services for Mark B. Putney, former president and bank chairman of First National Bank & Trust Co., have been scheduled for 7 p.m. Sunday at the Presbyterian Church of Richland social hall, 1087 Church.

Putney, who was 79, died Thursday at Borgess Medical Center. There will be no visitation.

The family has requested that memorials be made to Greater Kalamazoo United Way.

Putney, a resident of Hickory Corners, joined First National Bank, now called First of America Bank-Michigan, in 1922. He held a number of jobs ranging from teller to bookkeeper, rising to president and then chairman of the board in 1969.

He remained active on the bank's executive committee and board of directors until 1975.

Putney served as a trustee of the Kalamazoo Institute of Arts and was president of the Park Club.

A graduate of Kalamazoo Central High School and the University of Michigan, he was also a member of the U of M club.

Mark B. Putney

He is survived by his wife, Marian (Schoonmaker) Putney, and two children, Lynn Yates and Timothy Putney.

Arrangements were handled by Truesdale Chapel, 445 W. Michigan.

Norda's brother-in-law.

Close friend of Bob, friend and role model for John.

Mark Putney died 1984 .

Picture of Crete, location of hotel. Mark and Marian had restaurants here.

After graduating from Western Michigan University in June 1949, most of my 41 years being employed have been in the commercial banking business. The profession has been good for me in many ways. It was a respected profession and our monetary system depended on the clearing of checks and other money transfers through the banking system. For decades, saving and loan associations, credit unions and other financial service providers have relied on the commercial banking system to settle transactions. Now, with computers, the bank clearing system is not needed in the same way.

The public expected that banks were led by trustworthy persons. Ninety percent of a bank's funds came from the public, not the shareholders. It seemed to me to be important to be a banker and be in a profession of which a banker could be proud.

Many special events stand out as I recall those 41 years. Making sound commercial loans to businesses that had success was enjoyable, particularly to help start up new businesses.

Stewart-Sutherland Bag Company was one of my early fun projects. Bob Stewart grew up in Kalamazoo, with a father who was a police detective and a homemaker mother. Bob graduated from Purdue University and was enjoying a career selling paper products for KVP, a large paper mill located in the Kalamazoo area, actually Parchment, Michigan. One day he finally decided to start his own paper bag manufacturing business. He came to the bank to seek financing for this, needing money for a new imported German machine, other equipment and supplies and planned to start in rented space. Since his wife had some means, it was easy to make that first loan. Bob started having great success and L. W. Sutherland, a man on the bank board, heard of this success.

It just happened that at that time the consolidated Sutherland Paper-KVP Co. was considering selling to the Brown Paper Company, whose leadership was in Italy. Mr. Sutherland and his brother had started their Kalamazoo-based business and grew to a company that employed 6,000 people before it merged with KVP, which also employed many. Mr. Sutherland had a son in the business with high responsibilities but it seemed that he would not be a key player in the Brown Company organization. So, Mr. Sutherland offered to buy a half interest in the Stewart Bag Company so his son could join Bob Stewart. When Bob came in to tell me how much Mr. Sutherland was offering to pay, I was amazed, but Mr. Sutherland was much smarter than I. He had a career of selecting key men to be part of his large company. He judged rightly that Bob Stewart was a great one to over-pay at the start, knowing that in the end his son would do very well. He was right.

I was asked by Bob Stewart and Mr. Sutherland to be on the board of the new Stewart-Sutherland Bag Company and I did that. Other bankers would have jumped at the chance to buy stock in this new business that Bob offered me. However, my standards caused me to turn him down since I did not think it correct for me to be a bank lender of funds to a business that I partly owned - a conflict of interest. Some bankers would have agreed with me and most bank regulators would definitely have. The Company did prosper and in recent years I noticed a local bakery used Stewart-Sutherland bags in their business.

As the business grew, it soon needed more machines, supplies, people and space. Bob chose to relocate in nearby Vicksburg, and the only bank there offered him terms much more generous than our bank was willing to offer. We lost the business. I was on the board and could have owned that stock, but it wasn't offered again and soon, in 1972, I moved to Ft. Dodge, Iowa. Years later it was reported that Bob had donated one million dollars to Kalamazoo College, using Stryker Corporation stock, so I can guess that he did have much success before dying at a young age.

Another small business that I found a start-up loan for was the pharmacy of Jim Lefave. The events are fun for me to think about. He told me that he had approached Peoples Bank and Trust in Alpena, but was turned down by a man who left our bank for another position. I think I know what happened. It was a political decision, since Jim would be leaving the employment of a pharmacy owned by a former director of Peoples Bank. When Jim asked me for the loan I didn't need to consult with anyone else and this loan was easy to arrange. Based on looking at the expanded store and the new residence of the son, who is now running the business, this is a success story too.

As I enjoy having coffee and other things at McDonald's, it is fun to remember arranging for a loan to the owners of the first restaurant to open in Kalamazoo. The couple from Wisconsin didn't have much to invest but it did not hurt that she was related to Ray Crock, who started the whole McDonalds franchise in California. Charles Genite, who started the Alpena McDonalds, was a customer too.

In Alpena, an opportunity arose to receive an application from a new man to Alpena, Jim Phillips. He was a genius with machines and brought worn out automobile plant machines to Alpena, repairing them and programming them to modern techniques. Later he developed his own products. The business prospered for decades and only recently was sold to foreign interests.

I was associated with The American National Bank and Trust Company of Kalamazoo for twenty years and earned greater responsibilities as the years went by. For health reasons, I left and was asked to join Nazareth College in Kalamazoo as a vice president where I worked three years. Then I was vice president of The First National Bank of Ft. Dodge, Iowa, but within two years I was asked to join the Alpena bank under an arrangement that I would become President and CEO in three years. That promise was not in writing so events did not turn out exactly as planned. However, I had an enjoyable experience for many years. The bank was sold to a Detroit holding company, an outstanding organization.

The American Bank in Kalamazoo was founded in 1933, after the Depression, in the same tall building in Kalamazoo where there had been a bank. The officers had all worked at the previous bank, and an outstanding group of successful Kalamazoo men formed the original Board of Directors.

Most were still active in their own businesses, very wealthy, and felt honored to be associated with the Bank. Their interests were to have a safe, sound bank growing in market share with no emphasis on earnings per share. Their other activities provided substantial income for them.

Except for one young recent Western College graduate, all other officers had no college degrees, although some had taken courses in The American Institute of Banking, a nationwide school to give all bank employees an opportunity to attend classes, usually on bank time, and at no cost to the employees, except time to study. Classes in Negotiable Instruments were taught by local lawyers, lending by experienced current loan officers, and other subjects related to banking. I took some of these classes and later taught some. This program preceded community college growth in our country which

American National Bank Building

Nazareth College main building, now demolished.

probably caused the AIB program to lose its importance.

My first experiences were in auditing, so I was able to learn much about operating procedures. Then I was placed in lending areas; first in the credit department. This was where customer financial statements were analyzed and credit investigations made following the ethics standards of Robert Morris Associates, a nationwide organization that held regular meetings of lending officers, education programs and state and national conventions. All banks of some size belonged to RMA, but many small banks were not encouraged to be members. Nationwide, sound credit practices happened due to the use of RMA. Lending practices of recent years make me believe that RMA no longer exists since I retired in 1990.

When I was made Secretary to the Board of Directors I learned to know many of the Kalamazoo board members quite well and that was a big treat.

Soon after the new credit card service swept the country, another loan service was developed called "check credit". This was a system where a bank customer could activate a loan by writing a special check that had been pre-approved after an application had been submitted. At this time, savings and loan associations, credit unions, and stock brokers were not permitted to issue checks, so only commercial banks could offer this new service. We were anxious to offer this but we had a problem in that accountants believed we would have to charge 12 percent interest, and that rate was illegal in Michigan. However, after learning about this service in Chicago at an Annual Credit Conference, it became a personal challenge to figure a way to offer this before our competition figured it out, and for me, before my boss figured it out. The solution was easy. In Michigan it was legal to write a loan contract at a seven percent add-on rate. That is, if $1,000 was to be loaned for three years of monthly payments, seven percent multiplied by $1,000 multiplied by three, or $210, would be added to the loan or note, written for $1,210. My major in math at Western Michigan College gave me the answer. The real earning rate for the bank on this note was over the 12 percent annual rate that the accountants determined we needed to have a profitable service.

After preparing the documents to show others how this was the solution, my boss and I showed bank examiners what we planned and they approved. Next we drove to Detroit to show officers of the National Bank of Detroit, the state's largest bank, how to do this. We met in a conference which included their lawyers who said it couldn't be done. Well, they agreed that our method was legal and as we walked outside the bank, I thought I could jump to the moon. We were the first bank in the state to offer this new service. Applications poured in and we developed a large portfolio of these loans. In hindsight, our only mistake was to approve some weak credits for too much. As we advertised the program, we didn't want a worker to tell his friends that his credit had been denied so we approved most everything, knowing we had some poor credits. What we should have done was just to approve these poor credits for much smaller amounts, believing that they would keep that knowledge to themselves and knowing that we would write off their loans chalking it up to advertising. That was fun to have been the one to figure out the solution, a banking highlight for me.

The Kalamazoo bank experience permitted me to attend three summer two-week sessions at Rutgers University in the Graduate School of Banking.

This program required writing answers to problems during the year and finally to write a thesis, mine on "Replies to Credit Inquires," quite an undertaking. I also went to the Chicago Campus of Northwestern University during two summers for two weeks to attend a school on Financial Public Relations. Once again, we wrote answers to problems during the year and a special paper of our choice. These were great experiences and I met many very interesting and capable bankers.

Management of the Kalamazoo American National branching system became my responsibility when we had about fifteen. When we learned that the Allegan State Bank was for sale, we tried earnestly to complete the deal. If we had, our total deposits would have approximately equaled those of the First National, my uncle's bank. His bank started in 1865, and ours in 1933. We were ready to open a branch if we failed and the law required that a place we called "West Allegan" was an area that deserved a branch. To get around the law, banks would demonstrate that the number of residences, retail services, churches, schools and infrastructure legitimatized our naming "West Allegan" as a place, even though there was no government known as that and no notice of it on any map. We had a ready-made building which would be hauled in to open a new office. Mark won on buying the bank so we quickly opened our branch office. Immediately, Mark had our office closed, pending the determination in the courts if we were legal. Two days later, my boss and I were seated in a Grand Rapids court house and in front of us were my Uncle Mark Putney and Jim Duncan. In time, the court let us reopen.

As we promoted the office, we announced we were offering a free ox roast. Everyone was invited to come eat the meat and other things, hoping that in the process some new accounts would be opened. Not far from our office was the Allegan Forest and we soon learned that it was occupied with many folks that some would call "Cedar Savages", folks that were making their living hauling out the fallen lumber and folks with no extra money to open an account in our new office. They enjoyed the food.

Granting successful church loans was also fun. Because of bank experiences with church loans during the Depression, most banks had policies in the 50's to avoid loans to churches. At Rutgers University, I had a friend who wrote his thesis on "Loans to Churches" and he gave me a copy. Following this as a guide, we began making such loans and we made many. After our success, we put an ad in the Kalamazoo Gazette with pictures of the many churches to which we had made loans. The pressure following on the other banks was great so soon we were not the only Kalamazoo bank making such loans. That ad worked against us; we were greedy. However, prior to the ad, there was a time that we wanted to put a new office on property next to the rapidly growing Western Michigan University campus. A choice location was where there was then a church. I met with church leaders and, using some of the PR skills learned at Northwestern, I was able to convince them to sell us the property. With our being the only bank making church loans, I could assure the leaders that we would provide the funds for their new locations. That was fun because they made their decision that night and I almost jumped to the moon again.

One banking experience that I will not forget was our bank role at the time that the Upjohn Company decided to go public with a new stock offering. We offered our Trust services to be the transfer agent or registrar, I don't recall which. But, suddenly, there were thousands of new stockholders where there had been about four hundred before. Probably every broker in the country offered to get at least one share for their customers, but there was as much paper work to do for one share as for a thousand shares. Every bank employee, including the chairman of the board were forced to work every day for long hours just to keep up with this paper work. This was a new experience for our small trust department and the more experienced banks knew better than to assume this project. Naturally we got a fee, but once that project was completed the responsibility was moved by the Upjohn Company to a larger bank.

Another highlight for me had to do with a new computer system. Our first computer was a tape-driven IBM system. Then came the new disc-driven 360 IBM option. To prepare for this, I was sent to Detroit to be with a half dozen men from other professions to be team taught for one week by two talented IBM salesmen. On the first day, I thought I understood what was being taught, starting with the first binary number theory of it all. At the end of the day we were to write a simple program and take it to a computer. If the program ran successfully, we could go to dinner. I began trying to follow the example we had been given and what I thought I understood. Time passed, and I got nowhere. One guy from Toledo Glass Company left the room to go run his program, and I could hardly get started. After a while I heard another "student" ask for some help, so I jumped on board. When I was finished it was probably 90 percent work of the teacher and off I went to the computers. The program worked, and I went to dinner and it was late. We got to know the others pretty well, and one man had a key job in Alpena, which I had hardly heard of then. Frank Boynton was his name.

My uncle's bank, the First National, was also considering purchasing the new IBM 360 System. As I got thinking, it seemed to me that maybe we could form a joint venture and purchase only one system and that there would be other efficiencies for both banks. If we built a building to house the new system and had two separate, secure wings for each bank to prepare the data for entry to the system and have the results sent back to the separate bank wings this would be efficient. I prepared a paper with all the pros and cons that I could think of and took it to a competitor friend in the First National who had operation responsibilities. The feedback was that they were interested. So, a team of four, two from each bank, began a study traveling to New York to see an arrangement that already existed. On our team with me was Jim Walters, a brilliant man who had been an IBM salesman and a graduate engineer from the University of Michigan. My friend at the First National was the "generalist" of their team, as was I, but their technician was a senior converted banker, much inferior in talent to our man Jim. The leader and the one who wrote the report to recommend that we form the joint venture was Jim Walters. I remember the meeting with our team, my Uncle Mark Putney and my boss who decided that one more study should be done by a nationally acclaimed public accounting firm and one was hired. At the completion of their work they too recommended we proceed. A sight was selected, a building built in Portage, Michigan, and soon we were up and running. I was on the original board of the joint venture which did serve the banks well for some time. With holding company banks all over the state I believe the First National decided to open their own operating system a few years later. I was in Iowa when that decision was made, or at least in Alpena. Recently I saw a subsequent leader of the First National bank who expressed an opinion that a joint venture with a competitor was never meant to work, maybe he was right. (In Alpena, with seven competing banks, it seemed to work.) That man was instrumental in selling the First National Bank and he made millions doing so, although he too fired many career men who had been at the bank serving it well for many years. My uncle would not have been pleased with that successor. That has been the "big business" world of recent years, and that kind of greedy, selfish manner helped to really ruin the banking business in recent years, I think.

For eight years in Alpena, Joyce and I enjoyed the "perk" of attending annual Michigan Banker's Conventions at Mackinac Island and one year after dinner we had quite an experience. As we strolled near the water below the Grand Hotel we saw bright lights ahead and major activity. As we reached the commotion, it was clear some movie filming was happening and I stood next to a very attractive lady who was sitting on a stool swatting flies. Soon we recognized Christopher Reeve of Superman fame and then my new lady friend left her stool and went to him to shoot a scene for whatever film they were doing. The lady we later learned was known as Jane Seymour, an English actress whose first husband was the son of famous movie producer and director, Dickie Attenborough who did *Gandhi* and much more. She just turned 69 in February of 2010 and is currently marketing Kay jewelry. The movie being made was "Somewhere in Time," kind of a cult movie now.

So, banking let Joyce and me raise a family of four who all got their college degrees. At one time when three were in college we needed to get some loans which were all paid on time. We don't winter in Arizona or Florida, we do drive cars which have some age, but we have always paid our bills and made adequate community donations as well as church support. The work was fun and challenging and financially provided enough so we could do much traveling and get us through, as of January 2010, almost twenty years of retirement.

After attending a workshop in Canada in 1967, I became ill and was subsequently demoted at the American National and given a less responsible assignment. In 1969, I submitted my resignation to the bank and was given new opportunities in other professions. I chose to join Nazareth College in Kalamazoo as Vice President responsible for fund-raising, financial planning, Public Relations and acquiring new students. I will report on some of that experience later.

After three years, I decided to return to banking and joined the First National Bank and Trust Company of Ft. Dodge, in Iowa, as a Vice President commercial loan officer. This two-year experience was very enjoyable for me, but probably very difficult for the rest of the family, including Joyce. Then, the President of Peoples Bank and Trust Company of Alpena called to ask me to return to Michigan as Executive Vice President with the offer to promote me to President and CEO in three years. He planned to stay on the board as Chairman for five years when he would retire at 65, and disassociate himself totally from the bank and its Board of Directors. I never had a written work contract in 41 years of employment, having been taught that a person's word should be enough. This is one time that I should have had it in writing.

Alpena bank when I joined it in 1974.

OFFICERS		DIRECTORS	
GEORGE W. WILSON	President	FREDERICK T. JOHNSTON	HARLEY J. ENNEST
JOHN R. MILROY	Executive Vice-President	THOMAS McDADE SPENS	GEORGE W. WILSON
ROBERT G. BOYNTON	Vice-President	J. RICHARD WILSON	A. B. CROW
BILL McDONNELL	Vice-President	STEPHEN H. FLETCHER	DONALD GILLARD
DONALD A. LAWRENCE	Vice-President		
THOMAS R. GAPSKE	Asst. Vice-Pres. & Auditor	**TRUST DEPARTMENT**	
DAVID STEVENS	Cashier	RONALD T. OSTAN	Trust Officer
THOMAS B. WYLIE	Asst. Cashier	**ALPENA BRANCHES**	
DANIEL G. REISH	Asst. Cashier	F. JOE LaMARRE, Asst. Cashier	2nd & Ripley
HELEN K. HARRISON	Asst. Cashier	MADELYN MACKLEY, Manager	Miller - Oldfield
F. JOE LaMARRE	Asst. Cashier	**OSSINEKE BRANCH**	
LAWRENCE HIER	Asst. Cashier	ROD E. CHAPMAN, Asst. Cashier	Ossineke
RICHARD D. BOWEN	Loan Officer	**POSEN BRANCH**	
CHARLES KIMBALL	Mortgage Loan Officer	HARLEY J. ENNEST, Asst. Vice-President	Posen

Alpena Board at Cliff's Camp

Alpena Board and wives
at Temporary Park

Don Gillard in Mexico
with Bishop Bennison

My experiences in the banking business in small towns from 1949 to 1990 are the basis for this discussion about community service. Banking after the Depression of the 1930's until the 1960's, when bank regulations were changed, was an era of a respected profession, an important profession, and yet a time when bankers could have a lot of fun and also find time to be greatly involved in community service.

Our Monetary System required that banks be managed safely to insure the confidence of the general public. The Federal Reserve System of 1913 did not solve the Depression problems so it was determined that other new regulations were needed. Maximum rates on savings accounts and consumer loans were set and maturities of mortgage loans were established. Also, investment restrictions were placed so banks could invest in U.S. Government bonds and highly rated municipal securities, but banks had to avoid placing funds in the stock market and other rules were set as to how much could be loaned to those who were using the funds to carry stocks. The FDIC program was initiated in the 1930's to give confidence to depositors. Bank Board of Directors had to pass some "litmus" tests too, so they would be perceived as persons of unquestioned integrity.

Bankers should be reasonably intelligent, but not necessarily brilliant or even very smart, and probably most were not. Of course they should not be major risk takers or speculators. Safety of funds was of major importance followed by availability of funds and lastly came earnings for stockholders. Most stockholders didn't expect more than about 10 percent on net worth and no more than half of those earnings were to be paid in dividends. Bankers themselves didn't expect high salaries, but if they performed well, did expect that their jobs were secured, modest raises would be given annually and benefits would be good, including decent retirement pensions.

This was a time when "banker's hours" were actually short which left much time for involvement in personal activities as well as time to participate in community service.

During my twenty years of Kalamazoo banking I served as treasurer of the local TB Association, President of the Junior Chamber of Commerce, President of the Kalamazoo Exchange Club, and Treasurer of the Kalamazoo Chamber of Commerce. In the

United Way, I was President of the Board, Chairman of the Drive, and Chairman of the Budget Committee. Besides working on school millage campaigns, I was on the school board and President.

When I was asked to serve on a panel to offer proposals regarding the substandard housing problem that was well documented, I offered the LIFT Foundation, (Loan Improvement Fund, today) as a new program to help. While I served on other community boards and committees as well as much at St. Luke's Episcopal Church I still had my bank job and a growing family.

How could anyone do a competent bank job and spend all this time on these projects? That is a very good question. All of these outside interests had many committee meetings which often were held at early morning hours and at late evening hours, not just the time used during "banking" hours.

I have a theory about all of this. There were two major reasons that many bankers found the time for such community service. I have never read what I am stating; these are just my ideas, right or wrong.

First, due to the many governmental restrictions brought about due to the Depression, competition was restrained and it really wasn't that difficult to manage a bank. Maybe the business wasn't as it might have been in a more competitive environment, but it was not a difficult task. So there was time to do things outside the bank.

Second, often a positive response could be given to key customers to assist with their special projects such as leading fund campaigns to build structures at the local colleges, hospitals, senior citizen centers and more.

At this time, no interest could be paid on the large bank deposits held as demand deposits available by check. The owners of those funds felt they were entitled to more than a friendly smile as they entered the bank and an occasional lunch or dinner. These wealthy people were concerned about annual fund drives for Kalamazoo College or maybe the campus needed a new building. New equipment at the two Kalamazoo hospitals might be a concern. The Boy Scout Camp might need repair and many more great projects. The wealthy were planning to give substantially to these concerns they had but they needed people to carry the message, organize the campaigns, arrange for record keeping and much more. So the pool of bankers was there to come to their aid and after all, those bank deposits were sitting there and could be moved easily if the requested cooperation was rebuffed. These are just my thoughts.

However, in Alpena, the manager of sizeable government funds was not subtle at all in his request that the bank pay for a dinner for his employees to show our appreciation for his keeping the funds at our bank. It was illegal to pay interest on U.S. deposits in a bank. I wrote to our congressman to ask if there was a way for us to pay interest and the answer was a clear "No." I told our holding company boss that I intended to refuse the request to get around the law as requested and expected to lose the deposits as he found a more "pragmatic" banker to deal with. The boss told me my decision was correct and I told that manager who doled out Federal money for a living that we would not pay for his dinner or any other such project to "pay" for the Government deposits. He never did remove the funds, and within the year we have greeted one another in a friendly way.

Bankers did participate in community service and usually had fun doing so. Some bankers probably felt the publicity they received was good for them and the bank. If the bankers did a good job on the projects, there was a possibility that new customers would be attracted to the bank. I believe this gave opportunities to new young employees to mature as they carried out responsibilities in these projects. If a boss was one of those who was so insecure in his own life that he had to micromanage and take singular credit for all that happened at the bank that was good, and never gave much credit to his staff, then much self worth feelings could be generated for that employee as he or she participated in these outside community service projects. As I think back, I am describing what the work environment was for many of us at the American National Bank in Kalamazoo, Michigan.

The Junior Chamber of Commerce in Kalamazoo was a very busy organization for young men who were required to leave membership when they turned 35 years of age. I was not anxious to join the Jaycees, as they were called, as it seemed that many members were aggressive sales guys taken up with their own importance. But one day my boss who had been a Jaycee President suggested that I join and I did. It was a great experience. I learned to know many as great guys and good friends and I was later elected President. We followed Roberts Rules of Order at our board meetings and we held classes to teach these rules. We tried to trick each other, such as amending motions, amending the amendments and other technical things. But the basics were ingrained so we could lead a meeting and make sure that the minority was heard but the majority prevailed.

We got involved in a grass roots political project. We had a past local President who was serving as the parliamentarian at the executive committee meeting for the state Jaycees. He decided to run for President of the Michigan Jaycees and he was a popular candidate. There was a problem. The rules required that to be President you had to have been associated with that executive committee for six months and by election time he would only have been there for five months. So we would have to get the group to set the rule aside. But the Jaycee creed included something about "... government shall be of rules rather than of men."

We gathered a committee on a Sunday afternoon at our bank to discuss how to run the campaign and how to deal with this problem to make him a legal candidate. We planned to share attending local meetings to introduce our candidate and how to handle things at the annual meeting to be held in Lansing. We even selected key guys to vote against our motions so that they could move to "reconsider" an action.

There were several candidates and the rules required a two thirds majority vote to set that technical rule aside. It came time for that vote, and we missed our two thirds majority by two votes. For some reason, one of the other candidates moved that we recast that vote after lunch. We got on the phones and called several members in Kalamazoo to drive quickly to Lansing to make another vote in our favor. So, after lunch we had stacked the deck enough so our candidate had the two thirds majority and was now a legal contestant. Then at the election, he got about 90 percent of the vote. That was fun.

United Way efforts took much time for me. In 1960, I was Chairman of the Budget Committee. We met to be with board members of participating agencies and review written financial matters prepared by the paid staff of the United Way. We listened to statements from the agencies and what their request was for the next year. We had already been given an economic report as to what a fair estimate was for how much more could be raised. My duty was to introduce everyone, and they pretty much already knew each other, and to steer a half hour meeting with each agency. Usually this all went quite smoothly. But we had a racial problem with one agency.

During the First World War time, some white men had opened

a new service for black soldiers from Ft. Custer, and after the war the agency with its basketball gym, became a social and recreational center for the black families of Kalamazoo. While the white men and women provided the money and really kept control, they did put some black men on a token board. Most of these black men were waiters at the private Park Club of the elite whites. When WWII ended, young black men came home and they decided it was their turn to run Douglas Community Center, and they hired a new black man as the director and they removed the older waiters from the board. The white paid director of the United Way was used to really running things and he was not about to let the black agency director go against his wishes. When this agency presented its case to the Budget Committee, they talked, no questions were asked and their meeting ended. Then the United Way director told the committee all that was wrong. And, as committee members ate and drank at the Park Club, the alienated black waiters confirmed that all was not well at Douglas Community Center. What to do? Dan Ryan, Editor of the Kalamazoo Gazette, my friend and a great man, suggested that we employ Saul Alinsky from Chicago to meet with us and be a mediator. Dan was very left wing, and Saul had gained notoriety in Chicago assisting black families with housing and other matters. Dan planned to have his newspaper pay the bill. So, one day Saul arrived and we met at the Douglas Center.

In Saul's planned remarks he stressed that what we should have in Kalamazoo was "ward" politics. He said this is the only way that you can develop pressure to get things done for the underprivileged. When we took a break for coffee I said to Mr. Alinsky, "we don't need 'ward' politics in

Kalamazoo. We elect good people on our commission and they look out for everyone." He said, "Bull Shit. Who gets their roads shoveled first in your town?" Some of the ladies present who probably had never been at Douglas seemed shocked, but I thought; *Saul is probably correct.*

Later, I learned an interesting story about Mr. Alinsky. It seems that he had a project in mind for the underprivileged he was trying to help in Chicago. He needed Mayor Daley's help, the first Mayor Daley. He knew that he couldn't "buy" him, others had more money, and he knew he couldn't frighten Mayor Daley, so what to do? Then he learned that one thing Mayor Daley was most proud of was O'Hare International Airport and Mr. Alinsky thought up a plan that he had one of his aids tell to one of Daley's aids. At that time, planes were landing every two minutes and many passengers who were in need of using a toilet, found the plane facilities occupied, so they just waited to use the first airport facilities they saw. Alinsky's plan was to send bus loads of men and women to the airport and orchestrated a plan so that every restroom facility was occupied and lines formed so that no debarking plane passenger had any place to go. And the headlines of the New York Time's suggested might be, "Shit in at O'Hare International Airport". It has been reported that Mayor Daley capitulated.

In a 2008 book of Jerome R. Corsi, Ph.D. titled The Obama Nation, Leftist Politics and the Cult of Personality, he states that when Mr. Obama, after college, went to Chicago to lead community work, Saul Alinsky was his key mentor. The same book reports that one of Alinsky's prize pupils was Hillary Clinton and that her 1969 senior thesis at Wellesley College was a "75-page salute to Alinsky".

Another community project had to do with substandard housing that existed in Kalamazoo which resulted in the creation of the Lift Foundation, which was mentioned earlier but will be reported in detail in a chapter devoted to Racism.

Another project was a disaster from my view then, but with hindsight may have been a wonderful event for Portage, Michigan citizens. My views on this have probably never been written up by any other human being, and I could be wrong. But here is what happened.

One day I received a telephone call from Mayor Paul Morrison, a man that most of those I knew thought was a great person and a good Mayor. He said, "John, please come to the Holiday Inn tomorrow morning at 8 a.m. for a meeting which I can't take the time to explain now, but it is urgent that you and the others I am calling be there". With that approach I didn't think I had any other choice but to be present. So, the next day I joined a full house and at the front were all the city commissioners, the city attorney and the city manager - quite an impressive group.

Here was their story. They claimed that the Portage Township Supervisor was about to form a new city and its boundary would include much of the Upjohn Company real estate which, at that time, provided substantial tax money to help run the Kalamazoo City budget. The leaders said that we must head this off and we should all take legal papers back to our personal living areas to have petitions signed requesting the annexation of the Upjohn Company property into the City boundary. We were urged to rush to get this done and have all petitions presented to the County Building before any of the township petitions to form a new city of Portage could be delivered. Since time was of the essence, no questions were encouraged and there was no discussion. We blindly accepted that our leaders had the correct information and had thought through all the options, and out the door we went.

We were told that the number of signatures needed was based on the total votes that had been cast at the last election by both the city residents and the township residents. The percentage needed by both parties meant that only a small number of township signatures were required compared to that of the much more populace city residents. Well, guess who got the required number of signatures to the County first? And, in the recent past, reports indicate that the New City of Portage, Michigan, had over 40,000 residents with a median age of 36. Median income was $50,000 and median value of homes in 2000 of $120,000. The Portage City Government employed about 2,000 including about 300 part-time. The Portage School System had 3,000 students and it had two high schools. The households grew because many working at the Upjohn Factory and new office buildings decided to live near their work. Naturally, much commercial activity developed and restaurants and motels flourished. Maybe these results were meant to happen.

After WWII, in the Kalamazoo area, a trend was established of annexing political areas adjacent to Kalamazoo, so that its boundaries expanded. At the time of this action, many key employees at the American National Bank lived in Portage Township, the bank cashier, the head of the trust department and others. They had heard no rumors that the Portage Township Supervisor was thinking about forming a City, and gobbling up the Upjohn Company tax base. I believe strongly that the Kalamazoo City initiative was not needed at that time. If the Portage Township leaders on their own had started action to form a city, many leaders would have said, "Let's form a committee of City and Township leaders and study this to determine what would be best for all of us." There might have been a larger Kalamazoo with the annexation of Portage. I know one thing. Going about it as was done gave the whole Public Relations advantage to Portage Township. If the Kalamazoo leaders really wanted a new Portage City next door, it seems they made it happen.

This concludes a discussion of bankers doing much to try and make their communities better places to work and live in. Persons with no connection to banks spent a lot of their time and effort to work on good projects for their communities too.

During my first eighteen years, nothing major had happened to me in my mental and physical health. Even though we took shots, naturally I had the mumps, measles, chicken pox, winter colds and one operation to remove my tonsils. Never broke a bone, had a major fall, or was involved in any automobile wreck. What a very fortunate childhood.

When I entered the army I had no thoughts that I would be hurt or killed, especially since I was in the ASTP program which meant that the war would probably be over before I saw any "action". However, once I was in the Infantry and headed to Europe I began to have thoughts that I might not return. But as reported in the first Chapter, I escaped everything.

So, along came a surprise in the spring of 1967. I was given an opportunity to attend a Sensitivity Training Workshop in Canada, an event that my boss had participated in the year before as did Jim Duncan of the First National Bank of Kalamazoo and their reports were favorable. I was given a book to read, "Behind the Executive Mask" by Alfred J. Morrow, which described how a typical workshop was carried out. It sounded interesting and not too challenging. This was being sponsored by Western Michigan and Purdue Universities.

I boarded a plane in Kalamazoo and other participants were brought on board at some stops before we arrived in Canada. A boat was waiting to take us up the French River to Lunge Lodge on an island where there were cabins and a central building for meetings and catering. On the boat I began to meet the other workshop members, some from Michigan, New York, England and other places and all new persons to me. We arrived at the camp which was also accommodating several other men who were there on a fishing expedition. In the dining hall, our group was separate from these fishermen. We were divided into two separate groups; however each person in one group was assigned to a person from the other group. Then, each morning the couple met to discuss how each perceived what was happening. My "partner" was a married lady from Connecticut whose husband had a great job providing the couple with a luxurious home and more. She was an accomplished artist and had been asked to have many showings of her work. Our conversations each day were interesting. Well, something happened

Lunge Lodge FRENCH RIVER

LUNGE LODGE, CANADA, LAST WEEK OF MAY 1967

Flew from Kalamazoo 1967
to North Bay

to me so that by the time we left for home, I was encountering weird hallucinations and behaving in a not normal manner. I can remember some of the crazy thoughts I had and some of the crazy things that I did. As I got on the airplane, I was given a book to read called "The Territorial Imperative" a very studios work by Robert Ardrey, but what I thought I was reading was not what was in print and I was laughing on the airplane as I read - but there was nothing really laughable in that book.

To get to the airport, we were flown from the camp in a very small sea plane and in my right mind I would have been a bit nervous during that trip. We were driven by bus to the airport and I recall seeing a man fairly well dressed sitting on a park bench smoking a pipe, but he looked funny to me as his pants were hiked too high and displayed white socks that didn't fit with his dress suit and much bare leg showed. I had been smoking a pipe somewhat then, but seeing him caused me to throw my pipe away never to smoke one again.

When we arrived in Kalamazoo, Joyce was waiting with my friend Bob Rizzardi as they had been alerted that I was having a mental breakdown or something. I ended up in the psychiatric ward at Borgess Hospital in Kalamazoo and I recall more weird things that I did that caused the male nurses to put me in a straight jacket. While there, Fr. James Holt, our Episcopal priest that I knew well called on me and that helped a great deal.

Once out, I tried to work as I was receiving counseling but that did not work well. So, next I spent several weeks at Mercywood, a psychiatric hospital near Ann Arbor and Joyce made too many 200-mile trips alone to visit me. One Saturday she brought the boys and we all went to a University of Michigan football game.

Finally I returned to work, taking some medication to keep me functioning. Just before attending the Sensitivity Training Workshop, I had just been given a major promotion to be put in charge of all lending in the bank, commercial, personal and mortgage loans. Naturally there was much publicity about this locally, in Michigan financial papers, and even in National Banking papers. I was doing many other things too, service club, church work and especially the new LIFT Foundation promotion work with much speech making and I was President of the Kalamazoo School Board.

When this all started, I believe that I was on a career path that might have brought me to president of the bank, that is if our leader

At the monthly staff meeting Ray Wiskotoni, representing the Men's Bowling Team, presented the trophy won by the team to President Jacobson for the bank. Members of the team are: Ray Wiskotoni, Captain; Donn Hunt, Jon Van Emst, Denny Wiley and Dick Lindstrom, substitute.

The trophy is awarded to the high league team by the American Bowling Congress, "Airway Big 14".

Congratulations are in order -- may you repeat next year!

Our team is now entered as a champion in the "Champion of Champions" tournament on May 20-21.

JOHN R. MILROY

John R. Milroy, First Vice President, has been reassigned as Administrator of Loan Portfolios for The American National Bank and Trust Company. As such he will be responsible for administration of Commercial, Installment and Mortgage Loan portfolios, as well as American Security Charge and Loan Review.

John has been with American National since August of 1949, most recently in charge of all Banking Offices. He is a 1949 graduate of Western Michigan University. He is also a graduate of the Stonier School of Banking at Rutgers University.

John, his wife Joyce, and four children live at 141 South Prospect Street.

The new "360" computor is scheduled for delivery late in May or early in June.

This new equipment will temporarily be installed at our Burdick-Crosstown Office and should be in operation soon after delivery.

The "360" will supply the much needed time necessary for all the applications planned for our bank as well as time available for services to customers.

May 4, 1967

EXECUTIVE

APPOINTMENTS

Colorado
FIRST NATIONAL BANK, Colorado Springs: KENNETH E. BAIRD has joined the bank as assistant vice president in the commercial loan department.

Idaho
IDAHO FIRST NATIONAL BANK, Boise: Appointed are GORDON BAKER as escrow officer, head office; JERRY ANDERSON as loan officer, and KIETH ANDERSON as operations officer, Caldwell office; ROBERT D. GRAVES as installment loan officer, Pocatello office; EDWARD HARTMAN as loan officer, Rupert office; LARRY LEDINGTON as assistant manager, Wendell office; GARY LOCKE as assistant manager, Lewis-Clark office, Lewiston; LARRY MAUPIN as assistant manager, Shelley office, and GERALD L. TREBESCH as operation officer, Rigby office.

Kansas
FOURTH NATIONAL BANK AND TRUST CO., Wichita: W. DALE CRITSER has resigned as secretary but will continue as a director. HERMAN W. SMITH JR. has been named secretary.

Kentucky
CITIZENS FIDELITY BANK AND TRUST CO., Louisville: J. G. McPHERSON has been appointed vice president and continues as trust officer. Also named are WILLIAM F. SCHARFENBERGER as senior auditor; RENE B. ATZINGER as auditor; WILLIAM E. WUCHNER as assistant cashier, and ROBERT L. KOOP as assistant cashier.

Michigan
AMERICAN NATIONAL BANK AND TRUST CO., Kalamazoo: JOHN MILROY, first vice president, will become head of loan portfolios. DICK VANDERKLOK, vice president, will become administrative officer of communications and operations. JAMES LAMBORN and ROBERT VAN PUTTEN, vice presidents, will assist Mr. Vander-

On Thursday, April 27, 1967, Inman's at Galesburg was the scene of AIB's Annual Recognition Banquet. 185 students and guests attended the festivities. Guests included fellow AIBers from Grand Rapids and Battle Creek. Bill Rockhold, Associate Councilman for District 12, brought greetings from the National Office and Paul Root, Incoming President, gave a brief review of chapter activities for the past year. Highlight of the evening was the presentation of certificates for this year. Three American National bankers walked off with all the honors, as follows:

Ed VanderMey, Installment Loan Department received his Pre-Standard Certificate.

Jon Van Emst of the Trust Department received his Standard Certificate.

Tom Hamlin, Assistant Cashier and Manager of the University Office, received both the Pre-Standard and Standard Certificates.

The awards were presented by Harold Jacobson, President. Among the 1966-67 faculty members were Floyd Parks, who taught Trust Department Organization, and Jim Walters, who instructed the Fundamentals of Bank Data Processing course. Bill Rockhold announced that Barbara Burr, Assistant Comptroller, has been appointed as a member of the National Membership Committee.

New officers for the 1967-68 year include the following ANBers:
Ray DeVries - Second Vice President

decided to promote from within. I think I was ahead of the pack at that time. Besides being a First Vice President, I was still Secretary to the Board of Directors.

What to do? Our Vice President in charge of Human Resources was told to call on me and give me the Bank's plan and I must say that our president demonstrated his lack of "guts" by tossing this project away from himself. I guess I am glad that he was declared a 4-F and did not serve in the military during WWII. As I think of that, it is ironic that the man coming to give me the bad or good news, declared himself a "Conscientious Objector" during WWII and didn't serve either. This man had held a job at a local paper mill and near the end of his employment there he concentrated on keeping the business leader informed about the rest of the company managers. When he lost his job, I found him the job in our bank.

I was told that my salary would be lowered about 30 percent, and my title reduced, and my new assignment would be to start our first marketing department in a new office, far removed from any customer contact. I was assigned a new secretary and an extremely talented young man was also transferred to this new marketing department. Within a year this young man left the bank to join the Stryker Company where he did remarkable things and retired as a young man and with his wife donated a few million dollars to Western Michigan University who named a new Fine Arts building for them.

I struggled along in this new area and watched the addition of a new man to the bank who was the new "heir apparent". The pills worked and I got mentally stronger. Fr. Holt introduced me to a new book, called *I'm OK- You're OK*, written by Thomas Harris, a psychiatrist and these thoughts were of great help. This book discusses our three components of Child, Parent and Adult, and how we interact with each other depending on what is in control of each of us.

I had a great experience buying a new Olds Vista Cruiser using the thoughts of "I'm OK". My life-long discomfort with authority and power may have come about because I am too much in a Child, so a Parent type can take control easily and an Adult type can out-maneuver me. Here is what happened during this car purchase. On a Friday, I closed the deal with a salesman and returned to the bank all excited about the purchase. Then I got a call from the salesman asking that I come in Saturday to have my trade-in car reassessed because maybe he had allowed me too much. As badly as I wanted this new car, I thought a deal was a deal and shouldn't be changed. I was going to be an Adult in the next day's meeting, knowing that I might not get the new car.

When I reached the dealer's office, the salesman brought in two other men to talk with me after my trade-in had been assessed. The car was to cost $6,000 then and they only wanted $50 more, not much more really. One of the new men had played professional football for the Chicago Bears, and I had watched the other box as a heavy weight in the local Golden Gloves boxing tournament. Here were two huge, overpowering men. Was I intimidated? You can bet I was. But, I told them. "Look, if you made a bad deal yesterday, I am sorry about that, but we made a deal". They left to think about this more and returned and said they needed only $25 dollars more to close the deal. I said, "No, that would not be right." They gave in. They played their Parent roles well, I did my Adult role just as well and there was no Child around during this transaction.

I finally decided it was time to leave the bank with no idea what I would do next, but I felt very confident when I told the boss that I was leaving and was ready to leave that day if he wished. He just asked for a letter of resignation which I hand-wrote so he could not change it in any way. I had seen him change typed records. He said I could take 90 days with pay as I looked for a new job and that he would see if he could get me another bank job in another state.

When folks learned I was leaving, many new jobs were offered. Jim Duncan called to take me to Jim Gilmore, a prominent local man and their message was that a Vice President was needed at Nazareth College. They were both active there on the Board at Nazareth. After I talked with Sister Mary Bader, I flew to Minnesota to a small college to visit with the Vice President there about that kind of work; I returned and accepted the job with Sister Mary. Then, Jim Duncan called again and told me that he had a meeting with his key men and they wanted me to join the First National as the officer in charge of commercial loans. The nepotism rule that had prohibited me from joining my Uncle Mark Putney many years ago was to be ignored. Since I had accepted the offer at Nazareth, my ethical code said my word was my word so I joined Nazareth after thanking Jim Duncan. I will never know if I made the correct decision but I think the healing that continued while I was at Nazareth three years may have been needed.

When I broke down, Fr. Holt told our older children that I was wound too tight, like turning a clock too tight. I was involved in too many things for whatever abilities I enjoyed, and it just happened.

As recent as a 94th Division Association Reunion in 2006, some of our men stated that they had suffered and some still suffered from PTSD (Post Traumatic Stress Disorder) as a result of WWII. It would be a nice excuse to attribute my problem to that.

Before I left The American National Bank I learned about a University of Michigan professor, Dr. George Odiorne, Director of the Bureau of Industrial Relations. He was reported to be a strong opponent of all Sensitivity Training Workshops and had made speeches and written about this. He debated this with another educator at a conference at Cornell University. I wrote to Dr. Odiorne and he mailed me some material and told me that in his files he had many examples of individuals who had been harmed at the Sensitivity Workshop, including a high level automobile executive who committed suicide as a result of his attending the workshop.

In the debates, Dr. Odiorne's position was that there had never been any evidence documented that there had been any lasting behavior improvement in one person attending this training, but of course, he had much negative evidence. His position was that the training involved Group Therapy, "extremely powerful stuff, being conducted by amateurs." Dr. Odiorne is given credit for first introducing "Management by Objective" to the business world. He was much more than a routine educator.

Since leaving the Training Workshop, I learned from the lady artist that she was unable to paint for six months after the session. Also, the man from England wrote that his business life had been disturbed for many months after attending this session. While no study was done by Western Michigan or Purdue to determine any success because of the program, my records show that three of twenty attending had major problems subsequently. So, three of the twenty that participated, or 15 percent, was a rather high dropout rate.

As this is being rewritten in February, 2010, I considered leaving this out of the book since the college is closed and President Sister Mary Bader, when I worked there, died last fall and the major

I'd like to take this opportunity to call your attention in a very personal way to the Golden Anniversary Fund and its importance to the continuing development of Nazareth College.

We have in Nazareth College an institution whose concern and involvement in our city represents a great asset to the Community. As a result of their unheralded achievements in volunteer service and the nursing profession, hundreds of our fellow citizens have found richer and fuller lives. In addition, the dedication of the College to each of us has been matched by a quality liberal arts education provided to our young people for nearly half a century.

The Golden Anniversary Fund now provides us with the chance to actively involve ourselves in the continuing growth of Nazareth College. We have the unique opportunity of being shareholders in the future of both this exceptional College and our own community.

Great ventures always require a certain amount of sacrifice, but I am confident that once you have become familiar with what Nazareth College represents, your *commitment* will be as generous and enthusiastic as the *commitment* the College has made to all of us. The Golden Anniversary Fund represents a stake in all our futures, and I ask for your unqualified support in the coming months. We all have a great deal to gain.

Sincerely,

Jim Gilmore, Jr.

"Nazareth College is a Christian community whose membe are dedicated to scholarship, free inquiry, open dialog . . . who believe in the dignity, intelligence, strength ai sensitivity of the human person — male and female — the responsibility of each to develop his qualities to t fullest, not just for self-fulfillment, but for the contributic such development will make to each one's home, comm nity, country and world."

Sister Mary L. Bader, S.S
President, Nazareth Colle

buildings no longer exist. But some of the tales about people I learned to know there have just been told to me this year, so, I hope what follows is interesting.

A career as a college professor always seemed as though that would have been enjoyable. The closest that I got was when I was asked to teach an economics course at Western Michigan College when a professor had been recalled into the army during the Korean War. This one class met three days each week for one hour. I did my best but have no idea how the students reacted to my work. I do know that I tried to offer information outside of the text book but I stopped that after the dismal showing on the first test I gave based on their text book information. I assumed incorrectly that the students were reading the text book. Wrong.

Then, the very active banking program called The American Institute of Banking, which offered a varied curriculum, from Fundamentals of Banking, Investments, Lending, Economics to Negotiable Instruments taught by Rollie Huff, a local attorney. As students progressed they earned graduation certificates. At that time there was no community college in the Kalamazoo area. The banks paid the costs and employees were often permitted to leave work to attend classes. I taught several courses in this program. My new job at Nazareth College was not to be a professor, but what was offered sounded like a challenge.

At this time, Kalamazoo College, a very old liberal arts college and a great preparatory school for professional education, was well established in Kalamazoo. A well organized Annual Fund Drive received considerable local support. The student body was over 1,500 which met all year with arrangements for some education at European colleges. Kalamazoo College also had considerable endowment funds for this size school.

Nazareth College at one time had over 1,000 students, all women, but in 1969 enrollment totaled around 500. Also there was no established Annual Fund Drive and no cash endowment funds. Of course, the negligible salaries paid to the Roman Catholic nuns for teaching was, in effect, a type of endowment.

In 1889, the Sisters of St. Joseph arrived in Kalamazoo to manage Borgess hospital. In 1897, a new building was constructed to serve as the Mother house and residence for the Sisters. Later the girl's school to be called Nazareth Academy with a pur young girls to teach in their Catholic School System acros

In time the name became Nazareth College. Four years later, Barbour Hall was started as a boy's school and at one time there were 200 boys enrolled. After steady declining enrollment, Barbour Hall was closed in 1979. The Sisters of St. Joseph were also responsible for several other hospitals in Michigan.

For decades, a stone wall surrounded all the property of the Sisters and Kalamazoo residents were not encouraged to stop there, only if their daughters and sons were attending school there. Then along came Pope John with new ecumenical ideas and Nazareth decided to reach out to non-Catholic residents. Also, a major fund drive was held to improve facilities at the Mother House to provide for the increasing number of their aging teachers who would spend their last years there.

The funds developed were so substantial that the Sisters decided to build educational facilities and expand the Nazareth College campus. Three dorms of multiple stories were provided with connecting eating space and other beautiful rooms. A new air conditioned library was built that could easily accommodate over 500 persons. All buildings, including the multistory education and administration building, were connected by huge underground tunnels. I think this was a security decision to protect the female student body. Also, during winters and other inclement weather conditions, students, faculty, and others would never have to go outside.

When Sister Mary Bader was brought in as president she wore modern dress, although many Sisters continued to wear the traditional "Habit". Then the first male PR and Development officer was brought on board and he opened the college up, inviting Kalamazoo service clubs to hold meetings there. The stone walls still surrounded the campus, but Kalamazoo people were encouraged to enter. To help raise money for the college, a fancy dinner dance was held annually, the Nazareth Ball, with a big band brought in from Chicago. It was a gala that required fancy dresses for the women and tuxedos for the men, and young men were hired to provide valet service as the cars arrived in wintry weather. To be selected chairlady of this event and to be on the committee was considered quite an honor and received much attention in the Kalamazoo Gazette.

It became fashionable to hold wedding receptions at the college which had a beautiful room called the Georgian Room, with a place imported from Germany, and floors of inlaid wood.

The College Board of Trustees originally was composed entirely of the Sisters, but with the opening up to the outside world, lay men and women were placed on the board, some of whom were not Roman Catholics and the chairman when I was hired was Jim Gilmore, an active Episcopalian. The most prominent and influential men and women in Kalamazoo were a key pool for board membership. Also, the wife of one of the most affluent Kalamazoo men was on the board, as was a granddaughter of the founder of the Upjohn Company. Another Board member was from Owosso, the wife of a former U.S. congressman. These were all volunteer jobs but carried much prestige.

When I joined the college, I persuaded the auditor from the American National Bank to join me. He would become the business manager, replacing a Roman Catholic nun who had held the job for many years. Gordan Sleman was an active member of a Baptist Church. He and I did our best for three years and I think the financial affairs were a bit stronger due to our efforts.

I inherited a talented young man who would continue to carry out the publicity and much public relations work. He managed the printing of college catalogues and other printed materials. Efforts to try and secure new students were the responsibility of a man who had been in education and his task bordered on impossible. He traveled the state calling on Catholic high schools but the market was not strong for girl's colleges and growing community colleges created new competition for Nazareth.

We started the college's first Annual Fund Drive and did get the cooperation of many to make key personal calls for funds and we did raise $100,000. We sought grants from the government for the College's new four-year nursing BSN program and had some success, but there was much more to do.

In 1969, after I made the decision to join Nazareth, Joyce's brother Jon asked me to meet him when he came from Interlochen Academy to see his mother in Kalamazoo. When we met he gave me a very professionally done brochure prepared for a multimillion-dollar fund-raiser to build a new Interlochen College near Traverse City, Michigan. He specifically wanted me to give him the names of wealthy Kalamazoo persons that he and others could solicit for money for the new Interlochen College. This brochure had a full page picture of W. Clement Stone with his wife, he in tails and she in a beautiful dress. They were announcing a $5,000,000 gift to the

Drive.

In time, I learned that Karl Haas, the President of Interlochen was leaving to return to Detroit and reenter his musical broadcasting career. Then it was announced that the new Development Officer at Northwestern

University in Evanston, Illinois, was leaving his position as Vice President for development at Interlochen.

So, I got thinking, how are they going to raise the money for the new college at Interlochen with all of these key people leaving? As I looked at what buildings were to be built at the new college it occurred to me that we had most of those buildings already at Nazareth College. Then I thought if their new college took control of Nazareth College property and control of the college, which would no longer be called Nazareth but rather Interlochen College, there would be many other advantages to such a merger. Both were going to be liberal arts colleges. With the new emphasis on Fine Arts, student trips to Chicago to enjoy art and music there would be much more accessible than a trip from northern Michigan. Then, at that time students at Interlochen Academy were all wearing uniforms and the boys had short hair cuts. College age guys were wearing long hair and sloppy clothes. So having a new college next door would present a problem. Also, the instructors at the new college might think they were better than instructors at the Academy, probably not, but maybe.

The Nazareth Board of Trustees encouraged us to pursue this merger idea. The Sisters of St. Joseph were in agreement to investigate; only they wanted to be sure that their Catholic Order would have reversionary rights to all the property in case the merged college failed or moved elsewhere. That was reasonable.

Next we made an appointment with Eugene Power, a wealthy man in Ann Arbor who had an interest in Interlochen. Mr. Power started University Microfilm in 1938 and sold to Xerox after WWII and in 1971, he and his family donated money to build the Power Center for the Performing Arts on the Ann Arbor campus.

Sister Mary and I got in the car of our chairman Jim Gilmore, and he drove to Ann Arbor. We presented our ideas to Mr. Power who urged us to drive to Interlochen to have a discussion with key senior staff members there, who now were without a leader. Sister Mary and I went to Interlochen but these folks had no interest in investigating this merger idea. That was that, but in hindsight we probably should have tried to meet with W. Clement Stone, the man who planned to give $5 million for the new college.

In 1970, Interlochen hired a new president and later several more. The 5th, Mr. Richard O'Dell, launched a $45 million campaign which was exceeded. There has never been any publicity that a college was ever founded. Interlochen Academy and summer camp have been performing well and have great world-wide recognition.

In view of our weak financial situation, with Sister Mary's concurrence, a meeting was called for the Trustees to review three proposals. I first recommended an endowment drive for $5 million and at the least for $2.5 million. If neither was acceptable, I recommended that Nazareth College be closed. The Trustees chose a drive for $2.5 million and we employed Ketchum Inc, a professional fund-raising firm to help.

Then it came time to meet with National College Accrediting people at a meeting in Chicago, Illinois. Sue Parish was on the board, and just happened to be the granddaughter of the founder of the Upjohn Company. Her father was a brother of my friend Mary Delano's father, a Michigan State Senator. During WWII, Sue Delano, later Parish, flew aircraft for the U.S. Military, as a WASP.

In Kalamazoo, we boarded a small plane that Sue was to fly to Meg's Field on an island near the shore of Lake Michigan. We made the short flight, attended the meeting and obtained our accreditation. We returned to air space over Nazareth College and Sue buzzed the folks on the ground who were expecting us. Sue asked if we wanted to fly to Gull Lake so she could wave the plane wings at some friends there, and I said I wouldn't mind if we just got back on the ground, which we did.

A major change was about to be made at Nazareth since our Dean was about to be elected President of the Sisters of St. Joseph, and she needed to be replaced. I had an Episcopal friend at Kalamazoo College, Dr. Laurence Barrett, teaching then but had played a major role there earlier. As Dean of Kalamazoo College he was the leader to set up a new four quarter system which would result in the college facilities being used year round. He also led the way for negotiating consortium arrangements with colleges in Europe for study there. His success in all of this resulted in the Ford Foundation hiring him to assist in Higher Education for colleges in South America. He and his family lived there for a few years.

I asked Sister Mary to get him as a facilitator to meet with

Nazareth faculty to try and develop a new curriculum for the College. We were trying to compete with Kalamazoo College, Western Michigan University and a fast growing Kalamazoo Valley Community College. We needed something new to sell to attract more students, I felt. We did start this process, and I hoped that Sister Mary would invite Dr. Barrett to join Nazareth as the new Dean. I think he would have enjoyed that challenge.

The Sisters decided to continue the same curriculum and hired a Sister from another Congregation who was well educated but very traditional and I was sure no exciting new changes would be made. Gordan and I decided to return to banking and he got a job in North Carolina in auditing and I sought a commercial lending job, interviewed in Alpena, where a younger man would have been my superior, so I took a job in Ft. Dodge, Iowa.

My replacement was to be John Lore, then in Alumni work at his college, Western Michigan, in Kalamazoo. As he joined Nazareth, it was agreed that he would get his PhD in Education and be ready to become Nazareth College's President after Sister Mary Bader retired, and that happened. Not long after, The Michigan College's Foundation solicited John Lore to become the Executive Director of an organization which raised money for all the private colleges in Michigan. He took that job.

John called me one day to discuss starting a new fund raising effort in Alpena on behalf of the Michigan College's Foundation. We did that and he brought his father-in-law along. I asked a few friends to help make calls one day after a breakfast orientation meeting. We did this for two years only. While there, he told me some interesting stories about his experience at Nazareth College. I reported earlier that many Kalamazoo parents enjoyed using Nazareth College facilities to hold their daughter's wedding receptions. The fee for rent was low and the repair and cleaning up after many receptions actually caused a cash loss to the college. The good public relations of offering the college were not good enough to continue this practice. So, John got a Board policy passed to stop renting its property for all receptions.

Then came a time when a key aid to John Upjohn, whose wife was on the Nazareth Board, requested the use of the college room for his daughter's reception and John Lore said no, citing the board policy. This father thought he was important and that an exception could be made, but Lore said no. Then came pressure. First one of the most influential Roman Catholic men in Kalamazoo called John to request making an exception, and John said no. Then the brother, another prominent Roman Catholic, called and John gave another no. Finally, John Upjohn himself called on behalf of his aid, and John Lore told John Upjohn no. The reception was not held at Nazareth.

Later, John Lore received a telephone call from a Kalamazoo attorney who said, "I don't know what you did, but could you come to my office today?" John Lore said "of course". When he got to the attorney's office, the lawyer said, "Here you are," and handed John a several hundred thousand dollar check, payable to Nazareth College. John Lore believed that John Upjohn was very impressed at John's effort to keep the college functioning by following careful business practices and "sticking to his guns" and Upjohn demonstrated his feelings this way. The Upjohn family had already donated substantially to the college's $2.5 million campaign that had started before Gordan and I returned to banking.

Later administration leaders at Nazareth College added new athletic facilities for this college that became coed while Gordan and I were there. Unfortunately, never could enough students be attracted and the college closed. Some of the buildings were left standing and made available to social service agencies.

John Wooden, the famous UCLA coach, was once the coach at Indiana State University and he desperately wanted Harold "Hal" Gensichen to join him as a player. Hal was a senior then at South Bend Central High School in Indiana. In Kalamazoo, the coach at Western Michigan College was "Buck" Reade and he was recruiting Hal, too. Coach Reade was the winner as "Gence" or "Hal" as he was called, chose to come to Western.

That spring Hal was invited to be one of the All Stars, mostly college basketball players, to play in the annual Harlem Globetrotter basketball game in Kalamazoo at Western's basketball court. The Kalamazoo Gazette sports editor promoted this event mightily and there was always a full house of spectators. As good as the All Stars were, the Globetrotters could always win the game. Usually near the end of the game when the Globetrotters had the game won, they would stop playing real basketball and perform all kinds of stunts, which the fans loved. Well, that year the star player on the court was Hal Gensichen and the All Stars beat the Globetrotters. At the end of the game no stunts were performed by the Trotters. I think the fans had wished that Gensichen had not been such a great player so they could have seen the usual stunts. Rules required that Hal as a freshman could not play on the varsity team.

The following year, the Detroit Free Press designated Gensichen as the best college player in Michigan, better than stars at Michigan, Michigan State and all other colleges. Gensichen was a great player, not just a high scorer but quite a passer, many done blind and some bounced through an opponent's legs.

When I enrolled at Western, I got to know Hal quite well as we were both on the varsity tennis team that spring. We traveled with the team to meets at Northwestern, Notre Dame, Indiana and other places. I learned to know him as a fine person besides being an excellent athlete. WWII took him away from Western but he returned after the War and in 1947 put on a wonderful show as Western played the University of Michigan in Kalamazoo at the Western court that held about 2,500 spectators. This was the first time that any Big Ten basketball team came to Kalamazoo to play a game. The sports writer for the Kalamazoo Gazette wrote feature stories noting that Michigan star Pete Elliott would be guarding Gensichen and what a match up that would be. Elliott had already earned more letters at Michigan than anyone else combined in football and other sports he competed in. He was a great athlete.

I attended the game and watched Western win the game as Gensichen scored over 30 points, and in that era it was a high number. Unbelievable.

Fifteen years later, one of the other Western basketball players in that game told me a story which was later verified by other members of that team that I knew well. The story was this. After the game, there was a knock on the Western locker room door. It was opened and in came Michigan's Pete Elliott who asked to see Gensichen. As they met, Elliott handed "Gence" a jock strap that Elliott had worn in the game and said, "You faked me out of this all night so you might as well have it." Here is this great Michigan star demonstrating sportsmanship at the highest level.

At one time, Pete was the head football coach at the University of Illinois and his brother "Bump" was Michigan's head football coach. Their teams played each other of course in Big Ten contests. Later, Pete left coaching and then represented a Chicago firm selling products which caused him to call on my good friend Bob Rizzardi and architects in Kalamazoo.

In 1969, Bob Rizzardi did such a good job selling for a Michigan firm that they put their corporate airplane with two pilots at Bob's disposal and two architect friends of Bob and I were flown to Augusta, Georgia to spend the week watching the annual Masters Golf Tournament. One day as we walked the rough of the 17th hole, Bob spotted Pete Elliott and they all greeted Elliott warmly, Bob and the two architects. When I was introduced to Elliott I soon asked if he remember the 1947 basketball game at Western. He responded, "Do I ever, that guy really made a fool of me." Elliott went on to be the Executive Director of the sports Hall of Fame in Ohio. What a great sportsman.

Millions of men and women play the game of golf each year. If they only played the game for companionship and exercise and the thrill of hitting a great shot and sinking a difficult putt, that would be a great way to spend four or five hours. But when they decide to keep score and compete for prizes, then the trouble begins, and of course 99 percent of golfers do keep score.

Most golfers know the fundamental rules of the game, but when winning and collecting prizes and notoriety becomes the priority, cheating becomes the standard as I have observed many golfers playing over 70 years. The scores that most golfers report are really not accurate and if everything they did on the course was known, their cards should be disqualified. I still love the game and I loved to compete and score well, but I was taught the honest game and I played the game that way. My father taught me the rules. A CPA golfing friend of his told me that he could judge the need for close attention to a business he was auditing if he had played golf with that business' CEO and watched his ethics in the golf game.

The most flagrant violations of the rules are simple and few. The major golf cheating has to do with the improving of the lie of the ball. Usually the violation is only a small nudge of the ball to a smoother spot. Sometimes, I have seen golfers move the ball several feet to avoid an obstruction such as a tree in front of them. Balls are often moved away from a tree stump. Now, if the player wants to get a better lie, the rules accommodate this. Just add a stroke to the score, don't place the ball nearer to the hole and the distance to move it is in the rules. Most amateur golfers ignore this rule. Probably another 8 strokes would be added to the score if the rule was followed.

The only other major infraction has to do with putting on the greens. I actually never had heard of giving a putt because it was "inside the leather". I learned that in Alpena. Giving of putts is the other main problem since, by the rules, the hole has not been completed until the ball is putted into the cup. Just because the ball is very near the cup doesn't mean the player can do other than tap it in the hole. "Gimmies" are expected in usual friendly games and I have no problem with that if that is what the foursome does, to have fun. But if that is done, no scores should be turned in for handicap purposes and no prizes should be accepted and reports of scores placed in the local newspaper.

There are really many more violations regarding hazards, water, sand traps, "mulligans" and just plain courtesy matters that could be written now, but I just don't want to go into that in this draft. What difference does it make if a golfer reports a six rather than the eight he or she really took, when violation of the above happens so much?

When four golfers, most of whom never become very good at the game, have their fun trying to upset their opponents by making noise or in any way they want, that is OK with me. If they all are having fun, good for them.

William Jefferson Clinton has enjoyed playing golf, but it is well documented that the scores he told the reporters probably met his ethics in other parts of his life. Those who have watched and reported tell that when he hit a poor shot he would often hit another ball which, if hit better, is the ball he would choose to count for his score. It is a lot more fun to report taking a "Clinton" rather than taking a "Mulligan," and seems more American.

Author, Bil Gilbert, originally from Kalamazoo, has reported about a special kind of cheating that he learned about as a young boy caddying at courses there. One man was a real "hustler". Besides playing the game in his bare feet, no golf shoes, he taught selected caddies a trick to help him in his contests. At that time the cup in the green was metal and he taught the boys to bend the flag stick to gain leverage so the cup could be raised a little above the level of the green. The "Hustler" would give a nod to his caddy when he thought he needed this help to win a hole. If his opponent hit a straight, firm putt, the ball would still go in the hole, even if the caddy had raised the metal rim of the cup above the green level. But, a slightly off-line putt traveling at a slow speed would nick this rim and roll away from the cup. Bil Gilbert wrote me and named who that "Hustler" was, and I had heard of him, but Bil wrote that "he tipped well", which tells me that Bil was one of the few caddies that was taught the trick.

In 1982, Joyce and I won the lottery which gave us the opportunity to purchase tickets to the NCAA Final Four Basketball Tournament to be held in New Orleans. We stayed at the Monte Leone hotel in the French Quarter. At the games, our seats were so far from the floor that our binoculars almost didn't get the job done. However, this was a great experience for many reasons. It happened that the whole North Carolina basketball team, the coaches and many parents of the players were in the hotel with us. One time we were alone in an elevator with towering James Worthy and another time alone with Sam Perkins; we talked to both. After college, both of these players spent several years playing in the Professional Leagues.

That tournament was won by North Carolina as they defeated Georgetown. Freshman Michael Jordan made the final shot for Carolina and this was the first national win for Coach Dean Smith. Right at the end of the game, with time on the clock, Brown of Georgetown mistook a player to his side and passed the ball, only it wasn't a player on his team. That ended the game. There was still enough time for Georgetown to take a shot or get fouled, but the error cost them. With the game over, I focused my glasses on Coach John Thompson and watched him consoling his player. Two years later, Georgetown won the Finals at the tournament in Seattle, Washington, and Brown was still on that winning team. Several years later at the NCAA Finals in San Antonio, Texas, I saw Coach Thompson on the street talking to fans as they walked by. I went up to him and got to shake his son's hand, and then told him about our being at the 1982 New Orleans tournament and watching him console his player Brown. We talked about that a bit.

The next year we were fortunate in the lottery for tickets and we bought four tickets to the tournament in Albuquerque, New Mexico. We drove to Kalamazoo and then Mike and Tim joined us to board a train headed for Albuquerque. This was a new culture and geographic place for us. A special treat was that Joyce had an aunt and a cousin living there and we spent time with them.

The tournament was in a much smaller arena so we didn't need our binoculars as much as in New Orleans. In the finals, Houston was highly favored to win over North Carolina State, coached by Jim Valvano, but Valvano won. He died as a very young man and today money is still being raised in his honor to support cancer research.

In 1989, we bought four tickets for the event to be held in Seattle and again we planned to have Mike and Tim there. Joyce and I drove to the Regional Finals in Minneapolis, Minnesota, and then caught the train to get to Seattle with the boys flying in. We rented a car.

The tournament was exciting and Michigan beat Illinois in the first game and in the finals beat Seton Hall. With my sister Nancy living in Olympia, Washington, she invited us there and we saw sights in Canada with her. She also took us to the grave stone of General Robert Huston Milroy and we took pictures of us there. Due to the rainy and cloudy weather, Joyce and I never got a glimpse of the nearby mountains, but Mike and Tim saw them on their flight back.

Tennis has been a major part of my life since first playing the game in Kalamazoo at about age eight. Kalamazoo College had a great team with many great players, most from Kalamazoo, and Bill Culver from Grand Rapids. Marion "Buck" Shane of Kalamazoo was outstanding and often was men's champ for the State of Michigan.

In 1916, at Forrest Hills, New York, a new national and later an international tennis tournament for boys eighteen and sixteen was introduced to the world. The event moved to Boston and later to Chicago. Next it was held at the military academy in Culver, Indiana, where the tournament stayed for several years. Then, in 1941, the tournament moved to Kalamazoo College which still hosts the Tournament. The first year in Kalamazoo, new asphalt courts were built near the college's gymnasium and also near the New York Central railroad tracks. During the matches trains passed by and were not only noisy but often belched out much black, smelly smoke. This was quite a distraction.

At another time, a group of touring tennis professionals played some matches on these courts. About eleven of us young boys served as ball boys for the matches. Famous Big Bill Tilden of the U.S. played younger Fred Perry who was the best in the world then and he was from England. They played a three set match that Perry won. Doubles included them and Vinney Richards and one other. Tilden enjoyed being nasty to the ball boys and no reporters in that era reported that Tilden was a homosexual and at that time we probably didn't know what that meant.

Dr. Allen B. Stowe, a science professor at Kalamazoo College was the tennis coach and he was asked to manage the Junior and Boy's tournament, which he did for many years. Dr. Stowe had very poor vision so he was unable to play the game and could hardly teach his players. But he was a great recruiter and his teams were very successful. He also set up a shop in his garage near the courts and he earned money selling racquets and tennis balls and owned machines that his players could use to string racquets. In the summer, he ran tournaments and sold soft drinks on the side. Then one day as he was doing a routine walk from his home to the college campus, with his poor vision, he didn't see the car driving on Academy Street and he was killed on the spot.

My next door neighbor, Rolla Anderson, who shared a drive with me on Prospect, was the football coach and athletic director at Kalamazoo College. He was asked by the USTA to take over the management of the Boy's 18 and Boy's 16 Tournament that Dr. Stowe had been managing. A new stadium was built and named Stowe Stadium and the original surface was clay. One summer I had a job there preparing the surface by watering, rolling and putting white lines on the courts. In time, more courts were added using a hard surface and some of the viewing bleachers were covered with canvass for a shield from the sun. Rolla involved many people on various committees to help offer a fine tournament. Many Kalamazoo folks

USTA

— BOYS' 18 AND BOYS' 16 —

NATIONAL CHAMPIONSHIPS

AUGUST 2-10, 1980
STOWE STADIUM

KALAMAZOO COLLEG
KALAMAZOO, MICHIGA

1980

Program cover for USTA annual tournament 1980

hosted the players at their lake properties as well as the many parents of players who followed their sons to these and other tournaments. I played in this tournament once and was trounced by a young guy from California.

The Michigan Intercollegiate Athletic Association, MIAA, has been the sports league that Kalamazoo College was a member of. The schools were all small liberal arts colleges. It has probably been an organization for over 90 years. My folks took me to games played against Hope College, Adrian College, Hillsdale College, Olivet College, Albion College and others. In tennis, a coach for many years at Kalamazoo College was George Acker. Under his reign, Kalamazoo was the MIAA conference winner for 50 consecutive seasons, and he had one daughter who played professional women's tennis.

In Alpena when I arrived, George Thompson was still living and playing tennis as an older man whose eyesight was failing. Local rules caused us to not hit the ball too hard at George, especially if he was at the net. He played very well. Somehow I learned that George had driven to the annual Junior and Boys tennis tournament at Kalamazoo College for over 25 years when some of the roads from Alpena were not paved. I wrote to my friend Rolla Anderson, the tournament director, to tell him about George and I enclosed a small check hoping that it would cover a Kalamazoo College blanket or some other item. Rolla let me know he would do something. Then Joyce and I drove to Kalamazoo to watch whatever was to happen and George didn't know we were doing this. With a stadium filled with spectators waiting for the final match to begin, Rolla took a microphone and asked George Thompson to come down to the tennis court, and George did. Then Rolla told the crowd about George traveling from Alpena so many years and presented George with a plaque and gave the microphone to George for a response. While all of this was a big surprise, George spoke well and the crowd gave him a big hand. George was happy and so was I.

The highlight of my tennis career at Kalamazoo Central High School happened in 1942. Lee Koopsen, my doubles partner, and I won the Regional finals which sent us to the state Class A tournament in Ann Arbor. We made it to the finals but were runners-up.

In 1941, in the finals of the Regional Tourney, I had to play Bill Honey, who the previous year had won the Michigan Singles Class A Championship even though he played for a Class B State

High School. I recall our match vividly. Bill's dad was a prominent Kalamazoo professional man so Bill walked on the court with about three tennis racquets and he was dressed in long pants wearing a tan sport coat which I hoped he would remove before we started play. We had a good sized crowd. I was fifteen and played fairly well but my mind did not comprehend that I was about to defeat this reigning State champion. I didn't. In 1943, Bill and I were both on Western Michigan's varsity tennis team. Also on that team was Bob Stuckert of Milwaukee; an outstanding player. After WWII, Bob and his brother Wally were co-captains of Western's varsity tennis team and later, Wisconsin Men's Doubles Champions.

In 2008, when Joyce and I were visiting Casey, our granddaughter at Marquette University, I looked in the phonebook for Bob Stuckert. I knew Wally had died. A lady answered my call and I said, "Is this the home of the greatest tennis player that Western Michigan University ever had?" And she said, "yes and he is right here". I learned that Wisconsin had made him a member of their Athletic Hall of Fame in view of the numerous tournaments that he won in Wisconsin and all around the U.S. in tennis and squash. The computer details all of this. That was fun.

A Kalamazoo Central High School basketball highlight was playing on the same team with John Rapacz. He was a huge boy, still growing, and had success in football and baseball. In college, he was an All American as the football starting center at Oklahoma University with Bud Wilkinson coaching. Later John was selected as All Pro for his skill playing for the New York Giants. He ended his coaching days in Kalamazoo, at St. Augustin High School. A football stadium was named after him and a fellow coach.

When I entered Western in January 1943, I was a substitute on the freshman basketball team. One experience I will never forget involved a tough fullback of the football team, Art Macioszczyk from Hamtramck, Michigan. Then there was a traditional early season preliminary basketball game pitting the freshman basketball team against players who had won any letter at Western, be it football, baseball, track, tennis, golf or whatever and maybe these players had never played much basketball.

So, in this game I found that I had to guard Art Macioszczyk. I was about 120 pounds and not tall. Art was big and strong. My skills in basketball were primarily in passing, moving quickly and anticipating where   the ball was going. As I guarded Art, I stole the ball from him with my quick hands and anticipation. Great. But, it wasn't long before I felt a heavy collision with somebody and I crashed to the floor and I didn't see it coming.

As I looked up, I may have seen the smile on Art's face as he had retaliated successfully with this jerk, me, that had made him look foolish a moment earlier. After WWII, I played in this traditional game as a letterman against the freshman team which had a player I didn't learn to know for a year, my close friend of so many years, Bob Rizzardi. In that game I learned about Bob's competitive spirit.

In 1943 on Western's freshmen basketball team was Wayne Terwilliger, who became one of Western's greatest baseball players. After college he went on to star in professional baseball and near the end of his career was a coach in Minnesota. After WWII, Rizzardi, Wayne and I were in the group that Coach Buck Reade determined didn't have enough talent to play on the Varsity. So, we organized a team to play in the Kalamazoo City basketball league. Sergeant Fuel, where my dad worked, supplied our uniforms with the business name on our shirts. We had an interesting team that included some football hulks, the Schoolmaster brothers, and two brothers who had played well as high school players on St. Augustin's team and others. Coach Reade decided he had made a mistake by cutting Terwilliger so he was invited back to Western's team as a starter. I guess our city league team was pretty good. Oh, later one of the Catholic brothers ended up in Jackson prison and the other was pushed out of a Chicago Hotel by some unhappy gamblers, it was rumored. The Jackson prison brother was a ball boy with us for the Bill Tilden match and I played tennis with him a great deal.

We have held end zone season ticket seats for decades to University of Michigan football games. Before our sons married we often met them at these games. Now it is mostly Tim's family, especially since James graduated from Michigan State. For many years we traveled to away games, usually expecting the team to be successful. Trips to games at the University of Iowa gave us the chance to be with Jan, who still lives in Des Moines, Iowa. About the only Big Ten school where we have not seen a game is Penn State. We have seen some bad losses at Purdue and twice at Northwestern, none of which were expected.

In 2008 and 2009, we have not been happy campers and chose to avoid some games in Ann Arbor. In inclement weather I have no wish to make the trip to Ann Arbor and I doubt if we will attend many more away games. But, we have had a great time being in The Big House atmosphere and watching the Michigan Band practice and perform. The sights in Ann Arbor have been great, even searching for books at Borders, and as this is written, the only book store in Alpena, Walden Books, was recently closed by the owner, Borders. Ann Arbor restaurant experiences have been great, as well as fine arts opportunities there.

I have current golfing friends who never indulged in high school sports due to living locations, responsibilities on the farm and other reasons. One close church male friend has never had any real interest in sports. I can't imagine living those high school years without participating in sports.

This spring we plan to meet James and Lori in Indianapolis for the NCAA Final Four basketball tournament. Hopefully Michigan State will be one of the four teams. It was, and barely, beaten by Butler of Indianapolis.

Professional sports were of interest to me many years ago. Racing of cars, bowling, hockey, hunting and fishing have never been a passion for me. But, I cannot imagine a life that ignored all of the sport activities that have meant so much to me.

Today, professional football, baseball and basketball are of little interest to me. The players probably have more skills and stronger physiques than those of the era that I enjoyed. Today, the apparent arrogance of so many players gets in the way, as well as their lack of loyalty to a team, and there are just too many teams to follow. I should not be surprised, living in our free enterprise culture as we do, but the saying, "It's all about the money," may destroy many sports I believe.

UNIVERSITY AND COLLEGE GRADUATES

Iowa State University – Jan

University of Michigan – Mike

Spartan Stadium, Michigan State University Photo by John Penrod

Michigan State University – Jim

Western Michigan College – Joyce and John

Central Michigan University – Tim

WHEN WE ARRIVED IN ALPENA IN 1974, I NEVER KNEW I WAS TO PLAY TENNIS AGAINST THE "ACAPULCO CHAMPS"

THE ALPENA NEWS, Wednesday, April 12, 1972—

MEXICAN TOURNEY VICTORS—Dr. Ron Beatty and Dr. Dan Gulden (right center and right, above), along with the team they vanquished in the finals, quaff some of the champagne that was part of the spoils for the Beatty-Gulden victory in a tennis tournament conducted by the Acapulco-Hilton Hotel in that Mexican resort city. Vacationing with their wives, the Alpena dentists competed against other guests from all over the U.S. and Mexico and were the only entries not belonging to an organzied, year-around tennis club. Flushed with victory, the Alpena team accepted the challenge of the Hilton tennis professional, who chose an amateur partner, and proceeded to win that post-tourney match as well. In a victory statement, Beatty and Gulden said, "This trip was for our wives. We'd rather have gone skiing at Aspen."

LIFT – LOAN IMPROVEMENT FUND TODAY

In 1776, our founders decided to form a country where rights of each individual would be equal and where everyone would be treated as equal persons. It took about 150 years for women to be given the right to vote. It took about 200 years for legislation to be passed which attempted to give black people and women equal rights in education, job opportunity and more. About 43 years later, in 2010, racism, bigotry and discrimination are still problems in this country.

Has racism affected my life? The answer is no and yes. Since I am Caucasian, no is the answer. But, in view of things I witnessed, particularly regarding blacks, it has been easy for me to support their causes and to try and do something to help them.

Growing up in Kalamazoo, I was aware that there were not many black families living in the city of about 60,000, probably less than 1 percent. Most of these families lived on the north side of town, which originally had been settled by emigrants from the Netherlands. However, my first black friend, Gilbert McMickens, actually lived on the south side of Kalamazoo. His home was near marshes where celery and pansies grew. Hills south of his home rose to heights where many affluent people lived. Gilbert and I first met on the play ground before entering kindergarten and then we were in the same class until we graduated from high school in 1943. I was on the cross country team with him and he was about our best athlete. When we were competing in the State Meet in Jackson, Michigan, all of the white boys stayed in a hotel and we learned that Gilbert was taken to a private home. Hotels didn't accept blacks then. I don't recall that our coaches found fault with this, it just was the way things were in the 1940's.

Another black friend of mine was Willie Johnson, who did live on the north side of Kalamazoo. His elementary and junior high education was in buildings where most of the black children in Kalamazoo were educated.

In elementary school days, Willie and I started competing in track events, mostly the dashes, and in junior high we competed in touch football and basketball. There was only one high school building in the Kalamazoo system at that time, so all the black students were with the rest of us. When we graduated, out of 550 students graduating, there were only about a dozen blacks, who were called Negroes at that time. After WWII, Willie played basketball for his company team and we competed in the city league. I think that coaches in high school refused to let any black men play on the team. Willie's talents were such that he should have been on the team.

When I worked at the American National Bank, Willie would request a small loan which I always made and as he always paid them back on time he would say, "Thanks Mil," and that's what he called me. Willie was a very strong guy and competitive and always played by the rules, never took any cheap shots, he was just a great guy.

Bigotry and racism were not something I was too aware of growing up in Kalamazoo. As I traveled to Ft. Benning, Georgia, I saw the "whites only" signs at drinking fountains at the restrooms and other evidences that the world was different in the South. My barracks held twenty soldiers and five of them were black. We were all in the ASTP program which meant we were all "college material". Charlie Patterson was a black soldier who grew up in Ft. Wayne, Indiana. One day the two of us headed for the main base to get measured for the G.I. eye glasses that we both needed. The main base then was like a small city with restaurants, retail stores, professional offices and more. When we had completed our eye exam, it was noon time so I suggested that we go to one of the restaurants. Charlie hesitated and said we should go back to our Company headquarters, but I persisted, and we went in to a restaurant. Once in the door, a white employee came to tell us to get out since no blacks were allowed in there. I couldn't believe this. Here we were, soldiers on government property. We left and this bothered me a great deal.

Author Studs Terkel wrote a book called "The Great War," which I read many years after the War. He reported many much worse incidents on other U.S. Army bases. On one base there was one PX store for blacks with minimum inventory, and more than ten well stocked PX's for the white soldiers and were off limits to all blacks. There were five movie theaters for the whites and none for the blacks. Also, the blacks could see captured German soldiers, all white of course, who were allowed in the theaters and to purchase things at the PX stores. It happened that a black entered a PX and white soldiers kicked him in his eye. As other blacks started to come to his rescue, six trucks arrived with armed whites who surrounded the black men and started firing their guns. They killed some blacks and wounded others. This was happening on a U.S Army Base.

In Kalamazoo, Joyce and I had purchased the house on Prospect and had signs outside our Montrose Ave. current home. This street at the top of Westnedge Hill was a clean, pleasant place of middle income families. The homes were neat and clean and many occupied by Dutch folks who attended church regularly, some as often as three times each week. I started receiving telephone calls at work as well as at home with statements of "you would not sell your home to 'Niggers' would you?". One neighbor walked up and down the street telling others that our plan was to do that. That was how these good Christians really were.

In 1965, I was asked to participate in a Conference on Equal Housing to be held at Western Michigan University. Numerous studies had been done to prove that substantial sub-standard housing existed in Kalamazoo, occupied primarily by black families. Political efforts were made to deal with this and twice millage proposals were defeated. The Conference Committee first asked a senior Mortgage Officer in the First National Bank to be the banker at this meeting. He found a reason why he could not participate and he didn't offer one of his subordinates to participate in his place. I knew this was a black person issue, and since my sympathies were with them, I took on this role.

As we planned for the conference, we were told not to just talk about the problem but rather to offer some positive solution. At this time, Kalamazoo was being visited by Dorothy Kilgallen, a popular TV personality who was doing a story about Kalamazoo. Her city hosts took her to dinner at one of the best local restaurants, which happened to be located on the edge of some slum landlord properties which she couldn't help noticing if she was brought there in the day time. The heavy black population there would be evident too. Kalamazoo definitely had a problem to solve. What suggestion could I offer?

The North side of Kalamazoo was originally settled by white folks arriving from the Netherlands. Their houses were modest but very attractive, neat, clean and well maintained. Later as they prospered and were able to afford more costly properties, they moved to other locations, many to the south side of Kalamazoo. Then these north side houses were occupied by low income black families, mostly as renters, and slum landlords were born.

Another fact about post WWII that I learned about after graduating from Western and joining the American National Bank was the financial generosity of many Kalamazoo families. United Way drives, annual fund-raising for higher education and gifts to Bronson Hospital and Borgess Hospital were substantial. This was a time for many wealthy local people due to the success of the Upjohn Company, the successful paper mills, Checker Cab Company, Shakespear Fishing Rod and Golf Club Company and many others. The wealthy would decide that a new senior citizen resident was needed or more buildings needed at the colleges, or improved library and museum facilities. Often professional fund-raising firms were employed to lead these drives. The wealthy gave and set the standards and much of the rest joined in the giving.

Thus, my solution was to develop a fund of money which could be loaned on longer terms and at much lower rates than was available at the four commercial banks, the savings and loans and the credit unions. These loans would be used for home improvements to black families who were given an opportunity to purchase a north side house formerly owned by a Netherland emigrant family. Hopefully the land contract terms would be long term maturities and at reasonable rates so the young black couple could afford the monthly land contract and home improvement loan payments. That is what I presented to the conference held on a Saturday afternoon at Western Michigan University. I sought a fund of $300,000, not a huge amount in 1965. Next, with the help of the bank attorney, a new corporation was created called the LIFT Foundation, for Loan Improvement Fund Today. This non-profit corporation would receive donations that were tax deductible. To give confidence to the donors, I invited prominent local persons to be on the Board of Directors. The president of the Upjohn Company accepted, as did the leaders of banks and savings and loan firms. Various religious leaders came on board too.

Once all of this was in place, I started making speeches all over town starting with Chamber of Commerce breakfast meetings, evening church gatherings, noon service club meetings, everywhere. We set a date for people to give to LIFT and Congressman Gary Brown joined Senator Percy of Illinois in setting a LIFT TAG DAY. The giving began, and in time we could report that the fund had reached $300,000. Then we set up a committee which met weekly to review applications for home improvement loans.

145

SENATOR CHARLES PERCY BUYS TAG FROM CONGRESSMAN BROWN

Another group had been formed to develop government loans to create newly constructed apartment living for low income families. The two organizations merged and a director was hired. Some of the new housing was planned to be in locations which would make new integrated neighborhoods. All of this was happening in 1965, 66 and 67. With my illness in the spring of 1967, I had to back off my involvement in many activities, including LIFT, and I moved to Iowa in the summer of 1972.

In this same time frame, John Upjohn set up another organization to assist black men who wanted to start a new business or buy an existing one. John would provide monies and he asked several of us, bankers, CPA's and other business people, to be assigned to the new entrepreneurs as mentors for them.

The bakery bought by one man to whom I was assigned had been a very tasty store on the north side, started by a Dutch family. Whites from all over town drove there to purchase pastries. As the neighborhood changed, many whites feared driving there. The new black owner changed the menu and, unfortunately, he had a drinking problem in the early morning hours, so this business failed, and my friend and I could not be very good mentors.

Many years later I wondered if LIFT and the other activities were of much help at all. I am certain that there is still major substandard housing in Kalamazoo, and black folks and other non-whites exist there. I do think that something very positive happened. We had black and white men and women working on a positive project and many of us learned to know people of different color as human beings, which might not have happened in that era. The racial tension in Kalamazoo never became as it did in Detroit or in Watts, California. That was not our objective, but it was a good result.

Another unusual opportunity for me at that time was to give employment to the American National Bank's first black teller. She was the first black employee. At that time it was illegal for the state's unemployment office to keep records identifying racial matters. However, when the bank made the racial decision, I went to the State office. The State man let me see a list of a few names that he was not supposed to have and I knocked on the door of the residence where a young black girl lived. We hired her and not too much later, other black men and women were hired.

When we moved to Ft. Dodge, we found that the few black people living there were mostly working at a brick factory and there

JOHN MILROY (LEFT) RECEIVES CHAMBER OF COMMERCE AWARD
Making Presentation Is Past Chamber President Lee Stryker

C of C Honors Milroy

The Kalamazoo County Chamber of Commerce's annual Award of Excellence was presented today to John R. Milroy, Kalamazoo banker, for his efforts in the area of low-income housing here.

Milroy, vice president of American National Bank and Trust Co., was presented the award this noon during the 66th annual meeting of the Chamber.

Presenting the award during the meeting at the Holiday Inn-Crosstown was immediate past president of the Chamber, Lee Stryker.

In remarks prepared for the presentation ceremony, Stryker outlined the development of the Lift Foundation here, with emphasis on Milroy's part in that development.

"Lift was conceived as a revolving loan fund to be used by individuals to make major improvements to existing real estate under loan terms more lenient and at lower rates than loans available through conventional private lenders," Stryker said.

"Through the efforts of John Milroy," Stryker added, "The Kalamazoo County Council of Churches sponsored the program and organized fund-raising efforts."

He cited the work of other groups in the area of low-cost housing — including the Northside Development Association, Kalamazoo Housing and Improvement Corporation and the Interfaith Housing Council — and noted that the Lift Foundation was selected as the vehicle to carry on those efforts.

KALAMAZOO GAZETTE

Thursday, May 15, 1969   Section 2—Pages 17-32

Kalamazoo Chamber of Commerce award
from Lee Stryker.

148

trict were accorded a chance to view this fighting force firsthand and learn for themselves of their enviable record.

.... or several weeks a group of Green ....ta were stationed in New Hampshire's Grafton County where they underwent special cold weather survival training. While there they made a .... vorable impression on the residents, conducted themselves as good-will ambassadors of our Armed Forces, and left many friendships in their wake when they finally departed at the end of their training period.

As an example of the feeling these Green Berets left behind them, I am presenting here for my colleagues' benefit, the fine editorial from the Plymouth, N.H., Record. Its sentiments are typical of those expressed by New Hampshirites as the Green Berets left for duty in Vietnam:

TO THE GREEN BERETS

Whatever one's national inclinations, whether expressed through waving the flag, quiet repose or sincere difference, one thing is for certain; you cannot help but admire our Green Berets for the job they are doing and the group of men they are.

Here is a group of men who have volunteered for this special branch, each for his own reasons. They are given the duty of performing what is directed from above—our nation's leaders. Whether or not, in fact, they agree is subordinate to purpose. They are first United States soldiers.

We would like to think of a day when wars, armies, guns and killing would no longer be necessary but each of us knows inside, and especially these men in uniform, that this will be an awful long time in coming while a continue to struggle for power; some one criminal.

The United States, be it right or wrong and in a present-day context, still represents an ideal coveted by most of the peoples on earth—a nation governed by the consent of the governed.

We have our many failings, but at the same time like to feel we have fewer than anywhere else on earth.

The Green Berets represent this spirit of humility in many theatres through their devotion, comradeship, tolerance and the joy in doing a job. Whether jumping from a trembling aircraft for that exhilarating experience or rubbing frostbitten toes at the end of the day, these men are made for their job.

The education has been ours and we are thankful and honored for having had our area chosen. For whatever these men have learned about skiing, cold weather survival and snowshoeing, we have learned tenfold in seeing mind conquer matter and the joy in doing a job together, for the good of all. The departure of the Green Berets from Plymouth is unlike any other in years past for in those rumbling trucks go our soldiers and officers, our ambassadors, gentlemen, and most of all, our friends. In reality we must face the inevitable truth that some of the boys who have received orders to southeast Asia may not return from that teeming land. But the job they have done now stands out so much more vividly in our minds. In our own humble inadequate and Yankee manner we say Good-bye and good luck to the Green Berets of the White Mts. and the World!

LIFT: A Unique Proposal To Improve Housing for Low-Income Families

EXTENSION OF REMARKS
OF

HON. GARRY BROWN
OF MICHIGAN

IN THE HOUSE OF REPRESENTATIVES

Tuesday, March 14, 1967

Mr BROWN of Michigan. Mr. Speaker, In recent months members of both parties have begun a long-overdue appraisal of the housing problems in our cities and of our urban programs which have often failed to live up to expectations. As Senators CHARLES PERCY, JACOB JAVITS, and others in the Congress have pointed out: What is clearly needed is a fresh approach, some new catalyst by which we can benefit our cities and assist our low-income citizens by bringing them into a position of economic self-sufficiency.

In the last survey of housing in this country, in 1960, we had a total of 58.2 million units of housing.

The shocking fact was discovered that 10,952,000 of these units were classed as substandard, as defined by the Public Housing Administration. It was further noted that 826,259 owner-occupied units were classed as dilapidated, and that 501,352 units classed as dilapidated were standing vacant. The need for action in this field is clearly evident.

Last year citizens of Kalamazoo, Mich., recognized this need and implemented a plan to improve housing conditions for the less fortunate through a unique organization called LIFT—Loan Improvement Fund Today.

Conceived by John Milroy, a Kalamazoo bank executive and president of the city school board, LIFT is designed to fill the void which exists between low-income families and the normal commercial lending institutions. A private nonprofit organization, LIFT makes low interest home improvement loans to families who are turned away as "high risks" by the major lending institutions. Money for these loans now comes from the voluntary contributions of Kalamazoo County churchgoers. However, more substantial funding is anticipated from foundations and other interested groups as the program develops.

The first "LIFT Sunday" appeal in Kalamazoo County churches realized nearly $16,000. And LIFT "lifted" its first family a few weeks ago by providing the money for a Kalamazoo couple, unable to borrow elsewhere, to remodel the inside of their aged home. Since then, two other nonprofit groups—the Kalamazoo Housing Improvement Corp. and the Northside Development Association—have merged their efforts with LIFT to meet the housing needs for low-income families.

The combined forces of these organizations, with the support of the Kalamazoo County Council of Churches, are now staging another "LIFT Sunday" appeal, March 19, to accomplish their unified objectives.

I would like to take this opportunity to commend the citizens of Kalamazoo who have reached into their hearts to help some of the community's struggling families, and to urge everyone in the Kalamazoo area to again participate in this worthy cause.

For although this effort is presently small in scale and not a final answer to the need, it is refreshing to see a sound, workable program bring appreciable progress in eliminating urban blight without massive Federal spending.

It is also refreshing to see a program which puts the primary responsibility for better housing squarely where it belongs—on the shoulders of the community and in the hands of its concerned citizenry.

But more than this, Mr. Speaker, I hope that LIFT, and other programs like it, will focus attention on this pressing problem, and prompt my colleagues to bring out of this 90th Congress an effective and efficient housing proposal for low-income families that will lessen the burden of government, combat community deterioration, and provide the motivation to achieve greater human dignity and self-respect.

Veterans' Groups Endorse Veterans' Apprenticeship Assistance

EXTENSION OF REMARKS
OF

HON. CLEMENT J. ZABLOCKI
OF WISCONSIN

IN THE HOUSE OF REPRESENTATIVES

Wednesday, March 15, 1967

Mr. ZABLOCKI. Mr Speaker, I have been truly gratified with the response to H.R. 2383, the Veterans' Apprenticeship Assistance Act, which I introduced into the 90th Congress on January 16, 1967.

From across the Nation organizations and individuals have written to express their endorsement and support for the proposal. In some cases, the bill has been supported in principle, with suggestions for amending it.

In any case, this demonstration of interest is most welcome and signifies widespread concern about present inadequacies in the cold war GI bill.

As you know, Mr. Speaker, H.R. 2383 is designed to authorize on-the-job training and apprenticeship programs under the GI bill enacted by Congress in the 89th Congress.

The GI bill as it was passed in the Senate and introduced by many of us in the House contained provision for the inclusion of apprenticeship programs. This provision was in the tradition of both the World War II and Korean wars were few black families. The major employer was Hormel, and I am very sure that they had no black employees then.

At the Country Club in Ft. Dodge, there were no black members. Then a group of young men took over the leadership of the club. It just happened that occasionally on a stag day, a Hormel salesman would show up with a player from out of town who happened to be black. I don't know if he played well but his clubs and attire appeared quite expensive. The leaders of the club thought he was in Ft. Dodge on insurance matters and he was coming in from Chicago. The young new leaders of the club decided that this man should be the club's first black member. He was duly nominated for membership and accepted unanimously. Somewhat later someone decided to do further investigation as to the new black member's source of employment. They found that his real business in Ft. Dodge was to check up on the whore houses that he owned. The new Club leaders were stymied, and could only ignore what they had learned.

When we first moved to Alpena in 1974 there were few black people working or living here. I was told that not too many years earlier, a mayor set the rules that any black traveler should be told that it would be a good idea to be out of town before it got dark. I was told this, but I do not know if it was true.

On January 20, 2004, our U.S. Government issued a new postage stamp honoring Paul Robeson as the 27th recipient of its Black Heritage Series. He was born in Princeton, N.J. on April 9, 1898. His broad range of talents was evident in high school where he was an outstanding student and athlete. In 1915 he entered Rutgers College (now Rutgers University) on a scholarship and was the third African American to attend the school. He graduated as class valedictorian in 1919 and he was an All-American football player. He then obtained a law degree from Columbia Law College in New York. He joined a prominent law firm, but quit when a white secretary refused to take dictation from him because he was black. Then he became world famous using his speaking, acting and vocal talents.

The Alpena News printed a View Point about this new stamp. This View Point was first published in the Washington Times and had been written by Arnold Beichman of the Stanford Hoover Institute. This View stated that it was a travesty to honor Robeson this way.

In 1945, I was still in the 94th Infantry Division in Czechoslovakia. One day thousands of us sat in the field watching Bob Hope entertain

PAGE TWO

BEST BETS

To hear: There will be a new co-host — for a day, anyway — when Pistons captain Joe Dumars, right, joins Free Press columnist Rob Parker in the studio for "The Odd Couple" call-in show. (Regular co-host Mike Stone is off today.) The show runs from 2 p.m. to 6 p.m. on WDFN-AM (1130).

To see: Tuesday night at the fights? Live from Ledyard, Conn., it's Hector Camacho (49-3, 23 KOs) against Luis Maysonet (28-5, 24 KOs) in a 12-round welterweight bout on USA at 9.

Hall recognizes Robeson's football talent

A loose end in history was tied up shortly before Black History Month began, when Paul Robeson was elected to the College Football Hall of Fame.

Robeson, a Walter Camp All-America in 1917-18, received 12 letters in four sports at Rutgers. While working his way through law school at Columbia, he played professionally for the Akron Pros and Milwaukee Badgers in 1920-22.

But Robeson was best known for his singing and acting careers and controversial role in the civil rights movement. Accusations that he was a communist sympathizer long delayed his election to the Hall, which came Jan. 18.

Robeson, a 6-foot-3 end and menacing tackler, bottled opponents much of his life. In college, he endured a beating from teammates who did not want to play on the same field with a black man. His injuries included a broken nose, dislocated shoulder, split eye and numerous cuts and bruises.

Paul Robeson, at Rutgers

Despite that, he led Rutgers to a 22-6-3 record in 1915-18.

"I was the representative of a lot of Negro boys who wanted to play football and wanted to go to college," he said, "and as their representative, I had to show I could take whatever was handed out."

Robeson was a Phi Beta Kappa graduate and delivered the oration for his graduating class.

After graduation from law school in 1923, he worked at New York's Stotesbury and Miner law office, where he was the only black employee. When even the firm's stenographer refused to assist him, Robeson resigned.

He then redirected his talents toward singing and acting. In the next 25 years Robeson became one of the world's most recognized entertainers. Most notable were his lead performances in "Emperor Jones" and "Othello," which set an all-time record run for a Shakespearean play on Broadway.

A linguist who mastered 20 languages, Robeson sang spirituals and folk songs throughout America and abroad and played leading roles in 11 films. His most famous movie role came in "Showboat," in which he sang "Ol' Man River," still considered a classic performance.

Robeson also became an outspoken civil rights advocate. But charges of communist ties in the 1940s left him

stripped of his passport and stalled his career. The Supreme Court later ruled the government's action unconstitutional.

Robeson publicly opposed what he called "injustices to all minority groups," making speeches and benefit performances.

"Paul Robeson was a hero for black people because no matter how big he became he stayed grounded to his community, and that's an amazing accomplishment," said Dr. Melba Joyce Boyd, an associate professor of cultural studies at Wayne State.

Atlantic Coast Conference commissioner Eugene Corrigan, who heads the College Football Hall of Fame election committee, said of Robeson: "It became very clear he was an extraordinary person."

Robeson, who died in 1976, said of himself: "I'm just an ordinary guy like anyone else, trying to do what I can to make things match, to find and tie up the loose ends."
By Scott Talley

us. Later I was in a small high school auditorium listening to Paul Robeson performing and back in the States I read about him. I learned he was an activist and took a principled stand against racism in the United States. In the McCarthy era, Robeson was "black balled" in the U.S., which restricted his ability to perform here, and the politicians had his passport taken away so he could no longer perform around the world, where he was wanted.

When I read The Alpena News View Point, I typed a rebuttal statement and hand delivered it to the Editor. He did not print my letter. Then I learned from a Kalamazoo friend that The Kalamazoo Gazette had printed a great letter written by Roger Greely, a retired Unitarian minister in Kalamazoo. This letter congratulated our government on issuing the new Robeson postal stamp. I wrote another letter to the Alpena News suggesting that the paper print this Greely letter which was much better than mine. No response from the paper.

Next I decided to pay for an ad in the paper which was Roger Greeley's letter that had been printed in the Kalamazoo Gazette. First I called Roger to see if I had his permission to print his letter. Not only did he tell me it would be okay, but he told me a story about an event in Wisconsin. He told me that Paul Robeson was asked to perform in Madison, and when it happened, Roger's father was a practicing physician there. His father learned that after Robeson performed in Madison he was refused the right to spend the night in any hotel in Madison. Roger's father was incensed and let the community know that. Then, having expressed his opinion, he had lost about 10 percent of his patients and the Rotary Club that he was a member of shunned him for about three months. As they say, what goes around comes around. It happens that this editor of the Alpena News was a past president of the Alpena Rotary Club, and the anti-Robeson view might have been anticipated. But, wait. On September 15, 2007, the editor wrote a piece titled, "Setting the standard for racial harmony," so he has broadened his thinking. Great.

If we looked for it we could find much racism still in our country, but why waste the time. It is here and it may never leave the country. However, we did elect President Obama. He inherited a terrible situation in our country, and I am certain that the bigots hope he will fail.

This list of names could be much longer, but the question is, what do these men have in common?

Billie Sol Estes

Charles Keating

Bernie Madoff

Kenneth Lay

Charles Ponzi

Joseph, "Yellow Kid" Weil

Much has been written about all of them, and today, a quick scroll will tell many things about each of them. They were all "clever" men, and some spent time in jail for what they did to the public, some are there now, and another was headed there, but died first.

A commercial bank business lending officer is supposed to know much about the character of those to whom he or she is loaning the bank's money. Actually, all lenders, bank, savings and loan, credit unions - any lender must be trained to do a competent lending job.

In the 1950's one form of training was organized this way, and forget the poor grammar. The lender should ask himself or herself these questions:

1. Who am I loaning to?
2. What is the purpose of the loan?
3. What is the plan for repayment?
4. What is the cushion if all doesn't go well?
5. Does your experience make you feel that you are making a good decision?

The most important consideration is the first. Is the character sound, so you can trust what the borrower says? Is the financial data presented, honest?

Does the borrower have the experience and ability to do what he says? Verify, verify, verify. Know the borrower.

In my early lending years, I was very naive about analyzing character – I thought it was black or white. Either your word was good or it wasn't. You either had good character or you had bad character. If you are lucky enough to live on this earth many years, you soon learn that there are many grey areas. Too many business people buckle if there is enough pressure, or if their desires are pushed by greed, or whatever, and what appeared as good character at the outset may just not turn out that way. Character is not black or white.

So, would I have been able to make the right decision about dealing with the list of men mentioned above?

Bernie Madoff has made all of the others look like mere pikers. Reports are that he took billions from others, maybe $60 billion. He used the "Ponzi" scheme.

Billie Sol Estes was declared as one of the ten most outstanding men in the United States at the Junior Chamber of Commerce annual convention of 1952. He was caught borrowing money from banks based on collateral that did not exist.

Charles Ponzi became a famous swindler in the 1920's. He was born in Italy in 1882, and reportedly started stealing as a young man. In the United States, he created a pyramid scheme which made it appear to investors that they were certain to receive unbelievably high returns on their investments with him. What he actually did was to use new money being given to him as the source of the "interest" payments. He had no investments. Then, once his collections got large enough, he just ran away with the money. This plan was soon named for him as "The Ponzi Scheme". Bernie Madoff took this to a new level.

In 1974, just before arriving in Alpena, Joyce and I were in a Ft. Dodge theater watching the movie called *The Sting*. Robert Redford, Paul Newman and others were acting in the film. As I watched, I quickly thought I knew the whole plot of the movie because I had read a book written by Joseph "Yellow Kid" Weil and co-authored with W. T. Brannon. One chapter described the swindle that Weil perpetrated. Later that summer as I was in my hometown, Kalamazoo, I searched the city library looking for the book because that was where I had seen it. Nobody could find the book. Even my nephew worked there and he searched everywhere, to no avail.

After we had moved to Alpena, I had a business trip in Chicago and found time to stop at a downtown library and found that there were supposed to be two copies of the book. I asked a librarian to help me but the book couldn't be found. The librarian told me that this type of book was often stolen.

Next I asked the Alpena Library to search the State of Michigan and in time they found the book in the Michigan State University collection. I found the chapter that described the swindle used for the basis of movie plot of *The Sting*. I telephoned an editor friend at the Kalamazoo Gazette to ask if they still had a file on the Yellow Kid. They did, and they gave me his address at a nursing home in Chicago where he would soon turn 100. My friend also reminded me that the Kid had reportedly swindled the CEO and founder of one of the many paper mills near Kalamazoo. Rumor had it that this CEO tried to purchase every copy of *Real Detective Tales*, selling in January 1931, for 25 cents. The magazine told of the swindle of Jacob Kindleberger. In his book, the Yellow Kid states that a con man, such as he, can never swindle an honest man, because the swindle always has an angle that is either illegal, or at least very unethical.

When The Yellow Kid turned 100, magazines such as Time and Newsweek published stories about him, how many times that he went to jail and how he ended up under public care in Chicago as a penniless man. I decided to write a letter to the Kid suggesting that maybe Hollywood had swindled him if their idea for the movie came from his book. I didn't get a response, however I often thought that maybe an orderly passed word on to Mr. Brannon about the infringement. On February 26, 1976, the Yellow Kid died.

Soon, The Detroit Free Press ran a story headlined "Sting plot was swiped, author claims". The story said that a $50 million law suit had been filed by W. T. Brannon, the book co-author. The suit was against Redford, Newman and 12 others. Mr. Brannon died in 1981 and maybe there was a settlement out of court, but I have never seen anything further about this.

I got so wrapped up in this that I developed a speech to give to the Rotary and others, describing the various swindles of the Kid. I think it would be interesting for most people to read this book. For young people they might learn enough which will help them avoid someone's effort to swindle them.

At one time I knew a Dr. Tonken here. In recent years, a son of his wrote a book titled "King of Cons." This 38-year-old man reportedly wrote the book while he was in prison due to fraudulent activities. He was involved in fund-raising in Hollywood. He reports that his last major fund-raiser was to secure money on behalf of Hillary Clinton as she ran for the Senate.

Here are two more frauds that might have been avoided had there been any checking or verification about the persons:

The Episcopal Church of the United States could have avoided an embezzlement of $3 million dollars several years ago. The lady appointed to her financial job for the church was the culprit and she was married to an Episcopal priest at the time. Her resume stated she had graduated from a prestigious eastern college. One telephone call by the Bishop or one of his aides to verify things in her resume would have, or should have, uncovered her misstatements. Questions should have been raised with her before turning over to her the responsibility of managing millions of church dollars.

Ben Bradley, in his book about his job at the Washington Post, tells this story; As civil rights activities were flourishing, there came a time that he knew the newspaper should have at least one young, black, female reporter. So, he hired a young lady. In time, she wrote a series of stories about the problems of a young black boy and she won the Pulitzer Prize for her series.

Then it was learned that her story was all fiction. The award had to be returned and she was fired. Her resume also stated she had graduated from a prestigious eastern college and she had not. One telephone call to verify statements in her resume would have discovered the truth and she would not have been hired.

These stories go on and on. In 2007, Michigan newspapers carried stories about a Detroit investment expert who admitted she had swindled over $10 million from her customers. She also took three banks for a total of $23 million.

Sometimes it seems as if there are not a lot of successful, honest business persons. It is an enjoyment for me to have known Dr. Homer Stryker, an orthopedic surgeon of Kalamazoo. In the late 1930's, he started his business to manufacture various products that he invented. His circular hospital bed was one of his first. The business grew and finally he turned the management of the business to his son, Lee. I knew Lee fairly well, and I did some bank lending to the Stryker Corporation working with Lee.

Dr. Stryker developed a speech titled, "So You Want to go into Business," which I heard several times. He presented it in a humorous way, making fun of various government interferences, union matters and other things that surprised him. He gave the speech on Mackinac Island to a medical convention. Then came a tragedy. His son Lee was piloting an air plane in the Rocky Mountains and he crashed, killing all four aboard. When this happened, I was in Alpena. I have been told that Burt Upjohn and my friend Bob Stewart and others were asked by Dr. Stryker to find a new CEO. In time, they persuaded a very talented man,

John W. Brown, to leave an important job in the east and join Stryker Corporation. When Mr. Brown retired his net worth was reported to be over $1 billion dollars and each of the three grandchildren worth twice that much.

Bankers are supposed to be persons of integrity, since they not only are representing stockholders, but they are managing public monies. Too many have not had good character. In the late 1800's, the public learned about "wildcat banking." At this time, individual banks issued their own currency and some of it was sound and traded for face value, a dollar for a dollar. Some of the bank currency was of weak value and traded for less than the printed dollar. The latter stated that their currency could be redeemed for gold or silver but the location to do this was out in the woods and the place could not be found easily. These places were in areas where wildcats and other animals lived, thus the term, "wildcat banking." The National Banking act of 1865 was written because of this and other banking problems.

Another U.S. economic troubled era brought about passing of the Federal Reserve Banking System in 1913. This would supposedly prevent any future economic problems in our country and of course, it did not. The Depression of the 30's happened.

The collapse of much of our banking system recently must be attributed to greed, stupidity and no doubt dishonesty. Derivative investments are not understood by most persons and this includes many of our governmental leaders, elected and appointed, it has been reported. Paper connected to the housing lending market has been pushed by many unscrupulous business persons and reportedly encouraged by large financial institutions. Books report salesmen persuade borrowers to lie about financial statements and income. Debtors with basically no investment take on debts they cannot possibly pay. As of February 2010, I don't believe these problems have been solved yet, in spite of the government bailouts. Time will tell.

In the Alpena neighborhood, a county treasurer lost millions of county funds as he fell for a phony investment developed in Africa. The funds are gone and he is in jail.

To close this chapter, the summary should be this: It is true, "there is no free lunch." If it looks too good to be true, it probably isn't true. Know the people that you are doing business with and do plenty of verification if you are not sure.

There will always be "Yellow Kids," a Billie Sol Estes type, a Bernie Madoff when he learns about the "Ponzi Scheme," and many more. None of these guys will ever get you if you keep your greed in check.

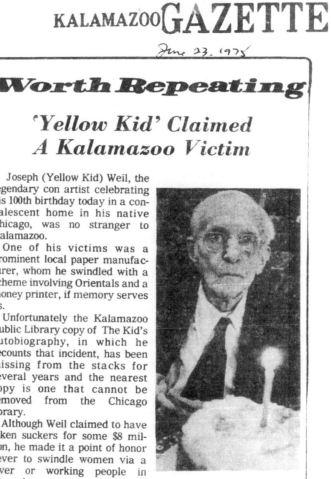

KALAMAZOO GAZETTE

June 23. 1975

Worth Repeating

'Yellow Kid' Claimed A Kalamazoo Victim

Joseph (Yellow Kid) Weil, the legendary con artist celebrating his 100th birthday today in a convalescent home in his native Chicago, was no stranger to Kalamazoo.

One of his victims was a prominent local paper manufacturer, whom he swindled with a scheme involving Orientals and a money printer, if memory serves us.

Unfortunately the Kalamazoo Public Library copy of The Kid's autobiography, in which he recounts that incident, has been missing from the stacks for several years and the nearest copy is one that cannot be removed from the Chicago library.

Although Weil claimed to have taken suckers for some $8 million, he made it a point of honor never to swindle women via a lover or working people in general.

"I never fleeced an honest man," he once said.

"Every one of my customers had larceny in his heart."

JOSEPH (YELLOW KID) WEIL
Swindled Kalamazooan

The Kid's special targets were bankers and big - money men. But he began his con - man career on a smaller scale, being arrested for the first time in a penny - matching "flim flam" game in Chicago in 1900.

Together with Fred (The Deacon) Buckminster he later set up fake handbooks such as the one portrayed in the movie, "The Sting," luring suckers with the promise of a quick killing in a fixed horse race.

Another of his more elaborate setups involved recreating the interior of a bank and then staging a fake robbery.

The Kid was almost as famous for his dress as for his swindles. A yellowed newspaper clipping describes him as

He swindled Kalamazoo prominent paper manufacturer.

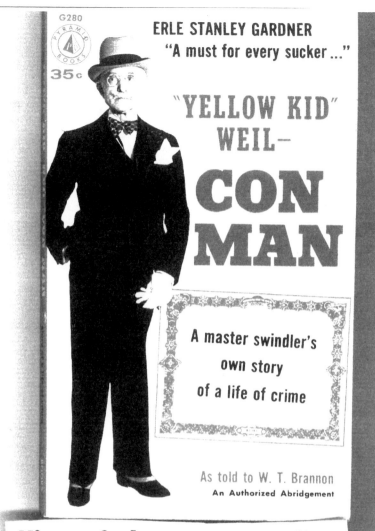

King of the con men dies

CHICAGO (UPI) — The Yellow Kid, king of the con men, is dead.

Joseph "Yellow Kid" Weil, perhaps the greatest con man the nation has known, gave the slip to a life of flimflam at the age of 100 Thursday.

He had spent his last years in a wheelchair at the Lake Front Convalescent Center, relishing a career based on the theory that you can't cheat an honest man but, happily, there's a sucker born every minute.

"A truly honest man would never have had none of my schemes," he once said. "I never fleeced anyone who could not afford to pay my price for a lesson in honesty."

The Kid figured that during his career, he conned his way into $8 million, mainly by duping businessmen, who wanted something for nothing.

"The Sting." Brannon contends the hit movie was stolen from Weill's life.

The Kid spun his life story often, usually beginning by saying, "I don't want to be a braggadocio, but ..." and then launching into descriptions of how he:

— Rented office space and hired lesser con men for a bogus "brokerage office," through which he worked a stock swindle for 20 years (his own wife believed he was a successful stockbroker until he was arrested in the 1940s).

— Rented an abandoned bank, hired pool hall characters as "tellers" and filled money sacks with slugs — all to fool a soap magnate from out of town.

— Tried to sell Cook County Hospital for $150,000.

Weill spent just six years in jail and he was hardly repentant.

"It was so fascinating that I didn't have

160

This chapter has been written and rewritten many times and I finally decided that nothing is to be gained by presenting the material as originally planned. If I had known that the "inside" problems were going to occur as they did, I never would have accepted the invitation to join the bank in Alpena. I should have anticipated that the bank would be sold before I had a chance to manage an independent bank, but the Detroit Holding Company that bought the bank was a "class" organization, and I was treated well by that company. The "inside" struggle from early 1981 to the end of 1982 never became public information except for what was said to a few friends of the guy who hired me, as he told them his version of events. It is possible that my need for a triple heart by-pass operation in 1988 and the case of shingles prior to that may have been triggered by the difficult times for me during the "corporate skirmish" and maybe not.

I am going to keep this little saga to myself and just chalk it up to an interesting time of my life. I was a "survivor" again.

Also, while the events seemed unusual and unexpected to me, what happened, probably happens routinely in all kinds of organizations. So, my tale could not be a fascinating one to read about.

I am glad that we took the job in Alpena. We were able to retire in the summer of 1990, after I turned 65. We have been able to pay our bills, donate to the church and for other things. We have enjoyed two great trips to Europe, and University of Michigan football games and basketball games. We have gone to 10 Final Four Basketball Tournaments, including the one in Seattle in 1989, won by the University of Michigan, and the recent one won by Duke over Butler University in Indianapolis.

I started attending 94th Infantry Division Association Reunions in 1986 as reported earlier, and those have been fun. Golf takes up time from May to October, however I haven't kept score for a few years now and I don't intend to start doing that again. We do "winter" in Alpena, and that has been okay too.

It has been fun watching our family grow to a gang of 15 and to be with them every year at Christmas time, and many more times during the years.

We hope to celebrate our 60th wedding anniversary on September 12, 2013, and our pills and operations have kept us going at almost 87 for me and 84 for Joyce.

Except for weddings, the most emotional religious experience for me occurred decades ago in New Orleans at an American Bankers Association annual convention. Thousands were seated in a huge hall as the chairman banged a gavel and introduced Fr. Frank Coco, a Jesuit Priest who would give the invocation. We sat back expecting a beginning prayer. Out on the stage came a six foot four black-suited man with a white collar, only he was carrying a black clarinet, not a bible. He stepped toward the microphone and began playing "Just a Closer Walk with Thee." The tones were beautiful, he was gifted, and the room was in hushed silence. I had chills running up and down my spine. When he finished, the applause was overwhelming, I think others felt the emotion that I did.

Decades later when I was with Kerry Redmann at a 94th Reunion, I told him this story about Fr. Coco. It turned out that some of the Redmann children had enjoyed Fr. Coco as their high school teacher in a Jesuit school. Also, the Redmanns often watched Fr. Coco perform in New Orleans night clubs, sometimes being asked to come out of the crowd on to the stage to play with Pete Fountain, Al Hirt and others. Father Coco died a few years ago, but I have read the book that he wrote about his life. I think if he were living and I was living in New Orleans, I would convert to be a Roman Catholic. Sister Mary Bader would be happy about that; she was when Kalamazoo's Jim Gilmore left the Episcopal faith to become a Roman before he was killed in a car accident.

NEW YORK

I have enjoyed some great experiences as I have traveled to this great city. Most times I arrived on the New York Special train from Kalamazoo, an overnight event. In the morning the train came south along the Hudson River, a beautiful sight. Three summers for two weeks as I attended the Rutgers Banking School, we would spend time in New York City. We saw the usual tourist sites, and a play if possible; *Music Man* was one of those. When Joyce attended the graduation exercise at Rutgers in the spring of 1958, we were able to get tickets to a new play, *West Side Story*. On Sunday afternoon, we rented a horse drawn cab to be driven through Central Park. We suddenly realized that the train departure time was approaching, so we hailed a Checker Cab after paying for part of the planned Central

Park ride and asked the driver to hurry to the station, and what a ride that was. Joyce was several months pregnant with Tim, but we literally ran to just get on board as the train was about to leave the station.

My trips to New York, as I was working at the Kalamazoo bank were all business related, but I could work in some fun. I really liked just walking around, and it was safe to do that in the 50's and 60's. I usually could get a ticket to a fun play – we sat up close watching the glorious Jayne Mansfield for example. I saw Pearl Bailey in *Hello Dolly*. She was married for decades to white band drummer, Louie Bellson and he had a brother living in Kalamazoo, Julius, who I often played tennis with. One play I attended was *Half a Six-pence*, staring Tommy Steel from England. It was opening night when I attended and I felt that the crowd was over-filled with part owners of the play. It seemed to me that the applause was much louder than you would normally expect for a dance number or a song, so the next day I was anxious to read what the reviews would say. Well, it was a big hit and was on Broadway for a long run.

One cold spring Sunday, I decided to attend a New York Yankee baseball double header in which Mickey Mantle would be playing. At the end of the first game I decided to leave, it was too cold for me. I got on the subway headed to the southern base of Central Park, I hoped. As I left the train and walked up to ground level, I looked around to determine if I was at the right place. As I was getting my bearings, I heard a woman nearby hollering at something or somebody. I spotted her, and she was headed my way. The next thing I knew was that she was hollering at me, "I told you never to come here, I will get that policeman to arrest you," she said, and there was a policeman nearby. She kept walking toward me and as she arrived, I turned, and she gave me a good swift kick in the butt. Well, I got the heck out of there, so that kind of ended my casual walk around the park. I suppose most people watching knew she was in her own little world and that I didn't deserve the kick. The policeman didn't do anything.

One time in New York, I was telephoning to make appointments to call on businessmen whose companies had deposit or loan arrangements in our Kalamazoo bank. The treasurer of a national finance company said, "Make your call at 4 p.m. and that should be your last call for the day." So I arrived at his office then. After some general talk for a half hour, he said, "come on; let's go out for a drink".

We walked down the street, to where, I didn't know. We arrived, and it was the Playboy Club, a new place for me. It was November, so we checked our coats, and headed toward some stairs. There was a "bunny" at the top, and she said, "Mr. Milroy, how are you?" I thought, *is this a Kalamazoo girl I used to know?* Then I thought, *my brother Bruce is in New York a lot, maybe she has me mixed up with him.* Naive, right? My host probably every day had a chance to play a trick on a guy from the "sticks" like me. As we had our drink, it was clear that all of the bunnies knew him very well.

Flip Wilson once was a very popular and successful black stand-up comedian, and could be seen often on TV. Naturally the censors on TV kept his material acceptable for family viewing. Once, a New York banker invited me to dinner and it turned out that the entertainment was to be Flip Wilson.

What a surprise for me. I was always looking forward to seeing him on TV and now I was to see him in person. The audience really enjoyed him, and I did too, mostly. But, with no censors to worry about, his stuff in the club was really dirty, *really* dirty. I am sure he started out this way and this is what the club crowd wanted, but I somehow thought he had risen above that. I was definitely wrong on this one.

Not too many years ago, Joyce and others from the museum here took a bus trip, first to Niagara Falls, then Kingston and New York and returned by way of Gettysburg, Pennsylvania. *Show Boat* was the wonderful Broadway play we got to see.

In Kingston, New York, we were encouraged to walk the downtown area in the early evening. As we walked by the courthouse, we noticed an historical marker, dedicated to Sojourner Truth. This is where this uneducated former black slave argued her case successfully for the return of her son from Georgia, where he was being held a slave, illegally. Having seen this, we made a point to read more about this woman, born in 1797 in Ulster County, New York, who became a leader in rights for women and minorities. Much has been written about her. Her last years were spent in Battle Creek, Michigan, where ten years ago a huge statue of her was placed downtown in a park. Her grave is also with a prominent marker and is in the same cemetery as the bodies of important Battle Creek persons, including the founders of the cereal companies there. A highway through Battle Creek is dedicated to her, also.

Battle Creek, Sojourner Truth and Me

Early in my Kalamazoo banking career, I was asked to take over a side job of managing Group Eight of the Michigan Bankers Association. This job was to organize two meetings each year, a spring meeting usually near St. Joseph, Michigan, and a fall meeting closer to Kalamazoo. At one time there was no Michigan Bankers Association, but there was a Southwestern Michigan Bankers Club. I learned from old minutes that the original group met for a fun weekend at the former Whitcomb Hotel, a place frequented by Chicago folks who were out for a "big time." The bankers brought in entertainment from Chicago and who knows what else. They went through the motions of electing officers and holding meetings. They probably compared notes on current problems and I hope didn't set any rates or other illegal things. They had fun for a few days.

When I was asked to take over, the job was to find a good speaker, arrange for a dinner, mail out notices and collect money for the tickets. The meeting now was to be a fun outing for all the bank employees of the eight counties in southwest Michigan, about 400 men and women. In the spring there was a golf outing for a few, and the others came for a dinner and entertainment.

One fall meeting, plans were to hold the meeting at the ballroom at Western Michigan University, and I had secured Madam Maria Paliski as the main speaker. I had heard about her/him from others. When I met "her" in the early afternoon, I took him to the hall to test the microphone and make sure he understood the arrangements. Then I took him back to the hotel so he could dress the part for his performance and arrange for a friend to pick him (now her) up at the hotel and get her to Western. He told me to sit him/her next to a man at the head table who might be classified as a "ladies man." At the speaker's table were officers of the Michigan Bankers Association, the State treasurer, Federal Reserve representatives, the State Banking Commissioner and others. I had to keep a straight face as I introduced the speaker to each of these men.

"She" spoke in a low, cultured voice, wore a drab black dress and began telling the audience about her background of Polish nobility. She was asked to be trained and serve as a spy for the Allied cause against Hitler. One night, she was dropped by parachute into German territory and it wasn't long before she became a friend of a Nazi Officer. She described this relationship and got to a point in her story when she was confronted by the Nazi who said he knew she was a spy. As I looked at the audience as she told this story I could see the folks were interested, but I had a difficult time not bursting out laughing as to what was happening. When she reported she is now known as a spy, she/he takes off his wig and begins spending the rest of his speech time telling the funny things that have happened to him as he went around the country giving this speech. I think I arranged for about 20 speakers, men like Earl Butz, former Secretary of Agriculture for the U.S., a former Minister of Finance for Hungary, a Southern Bank President who had been an All-American football lineman, and others. Madame Poliski was the most fun.

The Alpena artesian well is a symbolic story for a lifestyle of the past for this area. I learned early here that in many ways this is like a frontier town, and looking out for yourself is of primary importance. In business, "let the buyer beware," might have been the watch word for many here, who enjoyed a high profile and lavish lifestyle, but didn't worry about paying their bills and bank loans.

One day we were asked to loan money to a man who wanted to join others in acquiring some land for speculation. The group had a plan to entice others to construct a shopping mall on their property. Our borrower came in one day with panic in his eyes. He said their property was found to have an artesian well so that no shopping center could be built. Well, in time it was learned that once there had been a business property which had been burned to the ground. Except, only the owner knew that he had tapped into a water system and for years had been supplied with "free" water for his business. How much time was spent after the fire for the "free" water to be spilling into the ground to be learned, I was never told. The investors did sell the land and the shopping center was built. Today, half the space is not rented - I hope another fire doesn't erupt.

Two side issues at Ft. Dodge, Iowa are fun to remember...

The Chamber of Commerce decided to hold a several-weeks-long session to train business folks how to bring about change in Ft. Dodge. In an evening session, each week, professors from Iowa State University in Ames would present information. One night I recall, the professor showed how long it took for the farmers to accept putting chemicals on their fields. Another night was spent teaching us how to determine who the leaders were in Ft. Dodge or any city really. Then a night was spent learning about how city government works. At the last session, each participant was asked to identify an issue that needed to be changed. Then, each participant would see if they had learned enough to make their desired change happen.

The first winter I was there, our trust officer was the first to enter the program and at the conclusion he decided to get the local "dirty book store" closed. He began making speeches and going to ladies groups to let them know what was happening in their city. He carried a brown envelope, and when someone in his audience said, "What is dirty is all in the eye of the beholder," he would say, "Oh yeah, what about this," and pull some pretty scandalous photographs out of his brown envelope. Well, he got a committee formed including another officer of the bank to serve as treasurer. He started to make progress. But, then it "hit the fan." It turned out some very powerful folks in town were really behind the store, in business ways, and were making money. Pressure was put on the bank and the trust officer came close to losing his job. His committee disappeared. It still gave him money, but was willing to let this be his one-man crusade. The "dirty book store" stayed in business.

The next winter I attended, and my project was to get some tennis courts resurfaced and some new ones built. We formed a committee of tennis enthusiasts and determined that we could persuade the school board to go along. We succeeded, I am glad to say.

In Kalamazoo, I had been a Boy Scout and had passed all the separate tests to earn the First Class pin, but it hadn't been issued. Then I was asked to leave the program when several of us were caught horsing around in the church property where our Troop met. Then in Iowa, I was asked to chair a fund-raiser for the Ft. Dodge Boy Scouts. I said I would, provided they secured a First Class pin for me from The Fruit Belt Council in Kalamazoo, which was the name of the governmental organization for Scout activities there. Our fund-raising drive was a success and I have the official First Class pin and evidence that it was issued to me. Silly, eh?

When I was being treated at Borgess Hospital in Kalamazoo in 1967, I recall an interesting experience one late morning. Some social worker, maybe he was even a psychologist, was giving me the famous Rorschach test. He would show me a picture of something and I would begin telling him everything I could think of, and he would make his notes. My mind wouldn't stop producing thoughts. We had been at it awhile, and we were just getting started when suddenly I heard a voice outside the room. His buddy was ready for lunch and it was time to go. Off he went, never to return to complete the test. He probably was a sincere person but my case didn't interest him too much. Or, maybe he had already learned enough from my answers to know enough about what was troubling me.

Alpena General Hospital provided an interesting story for me. I was asked to submit my name to the County Board that owns the hospital as a potential Trustee and I was appointed. It was quite an experience and I was proud to watch the hospital success under the leadership of John McVeety. The hospital is now known as ARMC, Alpena Regional Medical Center.

This is a story about some false credit I received for possibly saving the hospital millions of dollars, as told by my friend, the late Dr. Peter Aliferis, once the hospital Pathologist. Peter was a bank customer and an ardent University of Michigan sports fan, and an enthusiastic human being. He was fun, and liked to hug everyone, other men too.

One Friday evening, key hospital staff and the board met in Gaylord with a purpose of brain- storming about hospital matters, and we were to let our thoughts "all hang out." An outside facilitator was there to steer the process. The next day I headed for Ann Arbor to see a University of Michigan football game. Sunday afternoon when I returned to Alpena, I stopped at the bank to see my mail which happened to include many papers from the hospital concerning a board meeting scheduled for the next day. On the agenda was the presentation by an investment advisor from Lansing for moving funds from Alpena financial institutions to deposits in out-of-state savings and loan associations to gain higher returns. My blood pressure rose. At the "let it all hang out" meeting in Gaylord, no mention had been made of this new investment thought. So, I came to the meeting prepared to ask questions about technical matters regarding savings and loan associations. I did that and the young man had no answers to my questions. Therefore, no decision was made to give the hospital authorities approval to transfer funds to the out-of-state S&Ls.

It just happened that at this time, major problems were reported in the S&L industry, headed by Charles Keating, who went to jail for actions he had taken with his businesses in Arizona. Soon we read about the "Keating Five," including Senators John McCain, Don Reigel from Michigan and three others. They had tried to intercede with government authorities on behalf of Keating. It wasn't long after that, the S&L industry blew up and we tax payers spent billions of dollars to save the industry, kind of like recently with the banking industry. Somehow, Dr. Peter Aliferis believed that I had inside information about this pending collapse and therefore protected the hospital by preventing the transfer of funds to S&Ls in the other states. I had no idea that this was about to happen.

When I began to hear the rumors of my great work, I didn't go out of my way to set the record straight, plus I was soon off the board as I recovered from my heart by-pass operation. I never have professed to be an investment wizard, and our life style proves that clearly.

UNIVERSITY OF OKOBOJI

More than twenty five years ago, the United States began to learn about the University of Okoboji, located in northwest Iowa. The founders were presented on the TV Today Show; the Wall Street Journal published stories about the University, and there was more. The 27th Winter Games of the University were held recently. This summer the 30th Annual Homecoming is to be held in the Dickinson County resort area, one of Iowa's top tourism draws.

In the early years, professors applied for jobs as dean or for teaching assignments in their special fields. The founders were Herman and Emil Richter who also were part of a family business located there. The store was formerly an implement store in 1960 when their father bought it and was named the Three Sons shop in Milford, Iowa. They sold name brand, fairly high-ticket sportswear.

The University gag started when the brothers kept being asked, "How are things at Camp Okoboji?" They thought about having some T-shirts printed with Camp Okoboji. That name was already taken by a real camp, so they created University of Okoboji, with an appropriate seal. This was put on wearing apparel, bumper stickers, fake foot-ball game tickets and fake honorary degrees. Their sports teams are the Fighting Phantoms, Herman is the director of student affairs and Emil is head cheerleader scout.

We have bought and worn some of this "University" garb. The Lake Okoboji area is a big tourist draw, and these men have had much fun and probably earned many dollars with their stunt. We stopped at the store one summer to find them clerking in their tennis wear and there was a clay court next door that they used when the store wasn't crowded. What a great spoof this has been. They set up a fund-raising foundation and reports are that the men have raised millions of dollars and donated the proceeds for projects like saving the local amusement park from the wrecking ball, building a YMCA and art center and financed popular community events. If it isn't clear, there is no Okoboji University.

It would be a terrible mistake to not write a bit about Joyce's family. Before we began dating in 1952, I had been at business meetings with Richard Petersen, Joyce's father, and observed him as a quiet, dignified, well dressed and kind man. Then when I was with him more, that original impression never changed. His primary hobby was to be out fishing or hunting birds when that was in season, and he did this alone since no one else in the family cared much about these activities. I did hunt with him once. Lucille, Joyce's mother, was a warm, kindly person whose primary interest was the well being of her family.

Joyce's brother Jon was an accomplished musician on the piano, and I first watched him perform in Ann Arbor, his senior year at The University of Michigan. Soon after this, Jon and his older brother Bob, who had graduated from Western Michigan in Kalamazoo, drove out west to seek their fortunes. We never saw Jon perform in Las Vegas and other places there, and he also was away from Kalamazoo, serving in the Military, arranging music for the Army Band. Jon met his wife-to-be, Evelyn, in Gary, Indiana, her home town, while she attended and graduated from Purdue University in education. Jon ultimately was employed at Interlochen, near Traverse City, and at one time was in charge of the music department at the Academy. Jon died in 2009, leaving Joyce the only one left of that family of five.

Joyce's brother Bob became a good friend of our sons, and our family had many wonderful times with Bob. While he did sales and office work in a retail store, his most fun was using his artistic skills painting and with other art mediums. When he retired and moved near Lake Michigan, he found us a house in the small village of Saugatuck which we rented thirteen consecutive years for a week in December. Bob celebrated with us each year before he died.

Joyce was raised by two wonderful, loving parents and had two interesting and enjoyable brothers. I was privileged to know Joyce's family.

CHICAGO

I should have devoted space to telling things about our fun in Chicago. With Mary and Bob Rizzardi, we learned about the Allerton Hotel when its Tip Top Room was the highest vantage point in Chicago to view the sights as we ate and drank. The Silver Frolics was a risqué place behind the Tribune Towers but it was torn down decades ago. The Michigan Avenue shops were fun, the Water Tower area and Rush Street places were great to see famous performers, singers, comedians and others. Then along came the higher Prudential building, followed by the John Hancock Towers, and finally the Sears Tower. Downtown used to be fun, especially in December when the windows were decorated at Marshall Fields, but that is history. The Metropolitan Art Center has been an important place to visit, and the foreign films, not available in Kalamazoo, were another exciting experience. Bob Rizzardi did business in Chicago so he learned about the many great restaurants. We enjoyed many of them.

When we moved to Iowa in 1972, our close relationship with the Rizzardis ended, but we have kept in close communication. After creating their family of three, John, Mark and Maria, they chose to part company and divorced. Bob remarried, Joanne is her name. They live in Ft. Myers, Florida and summer in northern Michigan near my cousin Dan Schoonmaker, who bought Bob's business. Dan has an airplane hobby and has flown Bob to Alpena and to Saginaw when I was recovering from the heart by-pass operation.

Mary moved to Point Townsend, Washington. Both John and his family are in Seattle, and Maria and her family live near Mary. Mark and family live in Minneapolis, where he teaches art in an inner city school.

In 1951, Mary, Bob and I were on our trip starting at Mary's family section of land near Comins, Michigan. One night we enjoyed the Knot Hole Tavern and the natives had fun with us explaining what the November deer season would be like based on their study of acorns and other vegetation. They probably were giving us a line but we accepted their words as gospel. Recently, the Tavern has made news in two ways. Not long ago, a tornado came through Comins and leveled many buildings but it turned out that one of the safest places to be was in the Tavern. I think a nearby church didn't fare so well. I don't think there is a lesson in that.

More recently I learned about the book, "Darker than Night," written in 2006 by Tom Henderson. This is a true story of a brutal double homicide that took 18 years to solve thanks to the great efforts of a Michigan State trooper who kept on investigating. A family based in Curtisville is reported to have been involved in all kinds of illegal activities and enjoyed starting bar fights in the Mio area. The book reports that The Knot Hole Tavern in Comins was a place where this family of men might start one of their fights. Two brothers of this gang are in jail for life, as the ones who murdered two innocent deer hunters who were up north to enjoy the deer season. After reading this book, I doubt if I will ever step foot in a bar that we might stumble onto, as Joyce and I enjoy driving back roads in northern Michigan. Before reading the book, on the way to Ann Arbor for football, I did take Joyce to the Knot Hole Tavern for lunch, but now I will never be in there at night, or any unknown bar to me.

We have enjoyed living in Alpena for almost 39 years, and much of the reason has to do with so many great people we have enjoyed. When we arrived, Tony and Agnes Skiba were still living and they produced a large family. In their last years, their daughter Helen Campbell lived with them as a widow and just this year the family homestead was sold to Roger and Rebekah Molnar. Having such great neighbors has made life enjoyable here.

In the Trinity church we began to know many well. Elbert and Audrey Heath enjoy being in groups, so they started the "Fryers Club." The couples of John and Betty Darnton, John and Cynthia Taylor, Dottye and Terry Carnahan and Joyce and I are the "Fryers Club." We were looking for the best Friday night fish fry and started at Smokey's Tavern near Hubbard Lake. The Heaths were from Wisconsin and apparently that state reveled in Friday night fish fries.

The church also brought us Joan and Ralph Lehner, the latter becoming a weekly eating friend. John and Ellen Eagan are buddies from the church. Ellen and Joan both had fathers who were Episcopal priests and the church still owns the rectory that Ellen was raised in, so you can bet she never wants the church to part with that building.

When we arrived in Alpena, the co-workers that were the most fun were, Bill McDonnell, Charlie Kimbal, Rick Bowen, Dave Stevens, Tom Gapske and Ron Ostan. Sue Serre Donnelly and Patti Tucker were my right arm. On the board then, Don Gillard and Ray Ballor were good friends along with Harley and Barb Ennest.

The new board members that I placed on the board were Cliff Anschuetz, Fred Wegmeyer, Steve Hier and Jim Lefave, and that was part of the Skirmish Chapter I will keep to myself, but it was very interesting, and they were great board members.

At the Alpena Country Club, there were four dentists; Ron Beatty, Dan Gulden, Don Coddington and Steve Hier who enjoyed first playing golf and then tennis. I became their first substitute, mostly because they wanted me on the tennis court. Before Coddington died, he asked the group to put me in his place, and then he died. In recent years, Steve Hier has dropped us for younger players and probably because we start too early and don't stay for dinner.

Jim Park has been my tennis partner and is a fellow Michigan sports fan and that is his alma mater. We have been at football games in Ann Arbor and would often see him among the 100,000 plus crowd. We have even seen him in Seattle at the NCAA basketball Final Four tournament when Michigan was the winner in 1989. In Minneapolis, when the Fab Five reached the final game, we met unexpectedly again.

This whole project started about ten years ago, and I began writing on yellow legal pads. Then in 2004, I decided I should be part of the crowd and bought a Dell computer, and that was a great move. That has made this project possible.

But Tim is the one who really got me started. He sent about 20 open-ended questions. For example:

Was General Milroy really a coward?

When did you first meet and date Queenie? Stories?

Details about wedding? Honeymoon?

What did you think of Hitler?

Memories of Depression? He meant the 1930's, not my mind.

Well, I think I have answered most of his questions, as I chose to answer them.

Of all the Alpena residents I have known, Rick Bowen has been the most fun to watch. He really should have been on the stage, with his wit, musical talents and style. But, he turned out to become a great banker in his personal loan specialty. He taught himself how to do his work well and he had the knack to be able to fit in with his far-away holding company leaders and he never was grounded on any harassment matters. I hope he and Nona have many happy retirement years, as Joyce and I have had.

Repetition is a good thing in education, but not in a book such as this. So, I hope I haven't already reported on "red-lining." For the past few years, much has been written about abuses in the residential mortgage market, and other abuses.

I think it was in the 80's, that the Federal Government decided that everyone was entitled to own a home, no matter where they lived or whether they could afford to or couldn't. Now, banks are expected to have sound loans if they are to be sound banks. Examiners always place strong emphasis on investigating the bank loan portfolio. If in large cities, banks knew there were certain areas which were run down and occupied by low income families, the bank could decide to avoid making loans in that area. The bank might even take a map and draw a line, a red line around that area so all their loan officers knew no mortgage loans should be made there. Then along came the government which declared that it would be illegal to have such policies, that loans must be made even though the odds were that the loan would not be repaid. How could a bank have a sound bank and be forced to make bad loans? Well, The Community Reinvestment Act was passed, and that unsound procedure became law. Every bank had to prove that it had no red-lining policy.

I drafted our new policy for our Board of Directors to pass. When they did, I prepared the minutes to read, Community Reinvestment Act and added Policy, whose acronym is CRAP, and that was typed in the minutes. I was curious if the examiners would take exception to this, but they never said anything. These past few years have proved that once again, the Federal Government and its leaders can be very wrong. This part of our economy is in a shambles.

KALAMAZOO

As an adult, I lived and worked in Kalamazoo for 23 years, and we have lived in Alpena for almost 39 years. Still, I keep my eye on my old hometown. This basketball season, the Kalamazoo Maroon Giants, as athletes have been known, were the Michigan Class A Champions. Something much more important is current stories about the success of the "Kalamazoo Promise." Five years ago, the world learned that anonymous donors had created funds to insure that all graduates of Kalamazoo Central High School would have tuition paid to any Michigan College or University that accepted them. To obtain 100 percent of the tuition paid, the student must have started in kindergarten and attended all twelve years in the Kalamazoo system. If the student only attended four years of high school, the amount is somewhat less, but still a great thing. Whether this is Upjohn-Gilmore, Stryker, or whatever money, we don't know. It is still an anonymous matter. Newspaper reports this month state that millions of dollars have already been spent on this wonderful project. Alpena is great, but I am very proud to be a native of Kalamazoo, Michigan, and "I have a gal from Kalamazoo, Zoo, Zoo, Zoo."

Lee and Jean Koopsen

Bruce,
John,
Joyce,
Nancy,
Marian

Bruce, Nancy,
John,

Aunt Marian in her 80's

Marian, Bruce,
Judy, Bob at
James' wedding

Joyce and John

My favorite picture of Joyce
in the fall at Prospect St.

Joyce at Victorian Tea

Joyce celebrating a birthday

Bruce, Aunt Marian, Joyce and me

Joyce, Jean and Lee Koopsen, Judy and Bruce

Jon and Evelyn Petersen enjoyed living at Long Lake as Jon worked at nearby Interlochen and Evelyn raised three daughters with Jon. She also was very busy writing a column published in the Detroit Free Press and other papers and traveled the United States helping with education projects.

Joyce with Jon – Summer of 2009 at Long Lake

Jan visiting Jon and Evelyn at Long Lake 2009

With Jan – December 2009

Mike, Casey, Kathy, Brianne – December 2009

Vicki and Tim with Elizabeth and Andrew – December 2009

Ellen, Lori, Jim, Erin – December 2009

Holidays 2014

EPILOGUE

NOW COMES THE FUN PART FOR YOU READERS...

ISN'T IT TIME FOR _YOUR_ BOOK?

The last four retirement years have been great fun for me. I have shared my book with relatives, past friends from hometown Kalamazoo, Michigan, army buddies and many new friends in Alpena, Michigan. This has been a ball. Books are now in about 25 states and a dozen foreign countries.

If I could finish **MILROY WAS THERE** with no formal training, but encouragement from key friends and relatives, and guidance from Angela Addington, Ed, Glen and Mary Jo of Model Printing, you can do it too. READY, SET, GO!!!

I started writing by hand with the hope that former secretary, Sue Serre Donnelly, could once again decipher my horrible handwriting. When she was injured, I decided it was time for me to enter the world of COMPUTERS. So in early 2004, a Dell device arrived as selected by son Jim. I audited two excellent classes on computers at Alpena Community College, and my high school typing training helped me hit the correct keys.

Son Tim gave me a set of questions that he wanted answered in the book, and Jan and Mike could start sending me e-mails. I knew the first chapter would be a brief report on 27 months of Infantry Service in WWII, but I had no plan for what would follow. I did ask for spelling and grammar help from a person selected by Model Printing.

When I finished a chapter, I mailed copies to friends and relatives seeking their reactions. The feedback was always great with comments to me to KEEP WRITING. No one wrote WHAT A BUNCH OF JUNK but just kept flattering me, so on I went. About 5 years ago, in 2009, I thought I was ready for Model Printing to print the book, there was about three times as much in a proposed book as I finally ended with. I did not like that finished material, so I destroyed the hard copy and deleted all in the computer. Time to start over and zero in on what I really wanted to say. I am so happy that the more concise version is what was printed.

The first copy was given to my wife Joyce in the spring of 2010, and she may have read the book. She has never commented on what she read in the book. In two months, we will have been married 61 years. Most reader reactions were very positive, although I was told about errors to have corrected when I got the next batch printed. At most subsequent printings there were other mistakes to correct. I think the current books being given away, have no errors to correct.

RECOMMENDATION NUMBER ONE

When you start, find a relative or good friend to play the role of a kind of editor for you. Ask this person to challenge you on detailed facts. Is the name spelled correctly? Is that the right spelling of a place and is the location correct? Even some grammar matters could be challenged. With this help, I could have made corrections early in the game. I should have been smart enough to seek this help early.

RECOMMENDATION NUMBER TWO

Kalamazoo native Bil Gilbert, an author of many books and hundreds of articles in *Smithsonian Magazine, Sports Illustrated*, other magazines and newspapers wrote me a long letter after he and his wife Ann Leander Gilbert had read my book, **MILROY WAS THERE**. His comments to me which will be printed below, should be of great help to all writers except those highly trained and able to write literary masterpieces.

Bil Gilbert died January 27, 2012 and on February 3, 2012, *SPORTS ILLUSTRATED* published the following:

"Died at age 85 of a heart attack, longtime *SI* writer Bil Gilbert. A renowned nature author whose wildlife stories appeared in *Esquire, The New York Times, Life, Time* and *The Washington Post*, Gilbert estimated at one point that he spent 40 days per year living outdoors; he even wrote a book—his first of ten—entitled **How Animals Communicate**. But, he became best known by venturing beyond the wild kingdom, first in 1969 with a three part series that represented *SI's* first substantial investigation into the use of steroids in sports, and later in '73, with a series on women's sports, which helped build support for Title IX and WON *SI* its first

American Society of Magazine Editors award."

When I learned that Bil and Ann had returned to the Kalamazoo area, I decided to mail them a copy of my book. I wrote, "it takes a lot of guts for me to mail my amateur status book to a skilled author, but here it is." His return letter is priceless to me, for many reasons, but the following quote might be of help to you new authors, at least I hope so.

QUOTE

"…As a genuine and considered comment from one who has been earning a living as a writer for sixty years: Very commonly avocational writers get what I think of as page fright similar to stage fright. When writing something for others to read formally they feel obliged to gussey up their prose, making use of frilly, fancy words and phrases.

The result is often something unreadable and ludicrous which obscures whatever it was they really wanted to say. *MILROY WAS THERE*, is a fine exception. *MWT'* prose is sharp, succinct, and therefore very readable. Is this a result of natural talent or have you been doing a lot of practicing?"

LATER IN HIS LETTER HE WROTE

"Anyway, *MILROY WAS THERE* stirs up a lot of good memories, gave us both pleasure and that is the true measure of merit for any book, John, you wrote a good one so thanks, and again, congratulations."

GOOD LUCK ON YOUR BOOK, AND HAVE FUN.
READY, SET, GO!

BOOKS:

Ambrose, Stephen E.	"Citizen Soldier"
Ambrose, Stephen E.	"The Victors"
Brokaw, Tom	"The Greatest Generation"
Brokaw, Tom	"An Album of Memories"
Byrnes, Lieutenant Laurence G.	"History of the 94th Infantry Division in World War II"
Corsi, Jerome R. PhD.	"The Obama Nation Leftist Politics and the Cult Personality"
Committee	"History of the 376th Infantry Regiment Between the years 1921-1945"
Eight Company	"Fifth Training Regiment, Army Specialized Training Program, Basic Training Center, Fort Benning, Georgia 10/25/43-2/5/1944
Eisenhower, John S-D,	"The Bitter Woods"; "The Battle of the Bulge"
Farago, Ladislas	"The Last Days of Patton"
Foley, William A. Jr.	"Visions from a Foxhole - a Rifleman in Patton's Ghost Corps"
Fussell, Paul	"Doing Battle - The Making of a Skeptic"
Indiana Library	"Copies Regarding General Robert Houston Milroy"
Jandova, Lenka	"The Stay of the American Army in Pilsen in The Year 1945"
Kershaw, Allexl	"The Longest Winter - The Battle of the Bulge and the Epic Story of World War II's most Decorated Platoon"
Mailer, Norman	"The Naked and the Dead"

Mauldin, Bill	"Up Front"
MacDonald, Charles B.	"Company Commander" the Classic Account of Infantry Combat in World War II"
Noyalas, Jonathan A.	"A Biography of Union General Robert Houston Milroy"
Paulus, Margaret AB.	"Papers of General Robert Houston Milroy" Four Vols.
Patton, George S. Jr.	"The War as I Knew It"
Powell, James R. Jr.	"A History of The Saint Luke's Boy Choir 1885-1985"
Prefer, Nathan N.	"Patton's Ghost Corps"
Pyle, Ernie	"L Brave Men"
Personnel XX Corps.	"Its History and Service in World War II"
Redmann, Kerry P.	"Unfinished Journey"
Standifir, Leon C.	"Not in Vain" A Rifleman Remembers World War II"
Standifir, Leon C.	"Binding Up the Wounds"
Terkel, Studs	"The Good War"
Terkel, Studs	"Hope Dies Last"
Toland, John	"Battle the Story of the Bulge"
Toland, John	"The Last 100 Days"
Thurston, Benjamin E.	"Ugly Duckling" 3rd Battalion, 376th Infantry Regiment, World War II Europe"
Turner	"Battle of the Bulge"
Wandrey, June	"Bedpan Commander" The Story of a Combat Nurse during World War II"
Whitman, Lt. Col. George Phillip	
	"Memoirs of a Rifle Company Commander in Patton's third U.S. Army"

Wood, Stephen B.   "On Being an Infantryman"

SPEECHES:

Manning, Charles Rev.   Twenty five or more speeches at 94th Reunions

DVD   "Patton's Ghost Corps."

DVD   94th Reunions and Boston Celebration of Mural drawn by Foley

YEAR BOOKS:

Kalamazoo Central High School

Kalamazoo College

Western Michigan College

MAGAZINE:

Stories of Louis Spitters, Bruce Thomas and Jack Briley

CHOIR PROGRAMS

St. Luke's Episcopal Boy's Choir of Kalamazoo, Mi.

Thanks to Angela Addington and to Ed, Glen, Mary Jo and the crew at Allegra Alpena (Model Printing Service)... I truly appreciate your help in the production of this book.